HAUNTED GLOBE

DEBE BRANNING

Haunted America

Published by Haunted America
A Division of The History Press
Charleston, SC
www.historypress.com

Front cover: The spirit of Sara Sorlin is seen at the Amster building. *Author's collection.*

Back cover: Welcome to Globe—the rear entrance to the 1916 Globe Train Depot. *Author's collection.* The Historic Gila County Courthouse and Jail. *Courtesy of the Bullion Plaza Cultural Center.*

First published 2022

Manufactured in the United States

ISBN 9781467150828

Library of Congress Control Number: 2022937936

This book is dedicated to Kip Culver, who helped create the Ghosts of Globe tour, and to all of the historians, paranormal investigation teams and townspeople of Globe and Miami who bravely shared their encounters with the unknown with this author.

CONTENTS

Contents

ACKNOWLEDGEMENTS

I would like to thank all the historians from the towns of Globe and Miami who graciously shared their knowledge of some of the most exciting tales of these historic mining towns—emailing me newspaper clips and photographs and pointing me in the direction of citizens with personal experiences. Molly Cornwell, Tom Foster and Lee Ann Powers were always supportive and answered my many questions so that these tales could be as historically accurate as possible.

A big shout-out to all the paranormal investigative teams, tour guides, tour companies and location owners who shared their experiences, data logs and stories of the unknown in order to fill these pages with the spooky phenomena they have encountered over the years.

A special thanks goes out to the late Kip Culver, who introduced me to many of the ghostly tales of Globe so many years ago. He painstakingly sat in his office to oversee one of the first overnight investigations of the old Gila County Jail by the MVD Ghostchasers in 2006. He never failed to message me whenever he discovered a new ghostly historic tale concerning the jail—somehow, I know he would be excited about this book.

I thank my paranormal team and personal paranormal friends who have accompanied me to explore the spirits and mysteries of Globe and Miami. Kudos to all who helped with photography and edits to the manuscript.

Again, my wish is for other paranormal enthusiasts to hop in their vehicles and explore the spirits encountered in these old mining towns before they are a misty memory of the past. And as always, I will add, "History and mystery go hand in hand!" Carry on the tradition!

INTRODUCTION

The town of Globe, Arizona, known today for its copper mining, began as a prosperous silver mining town. Silver brought in eager prospectors and mining expeditions. It was after the Civil War, and men were making their way west to get rich quick. Their search for precious metals such as gold and silver helped create many of the mining communities in the area we know today.

Silver was discovered near Alice Gulch and Pinal Creek in 1873. Miners and prospectors established the small camp there that soon became known as Globe City. Folks congregated to the new mining camp, settling along Pinal Creek, just south of the original camp. They arrived from countries all over the world—Italy, Germany, Mexico, Croatia, China, Ireland and more. Globe became a giant melting pot of all nationalities and ethnic groups working together to build a great city. The settlement was renamed Globe in 1876, the same year that the Globe Post Office was established. By the 1880s, there were over one thousand people residing in Globe and its hills and vast canyons.

Sadly, the silver lodes began to play out within the town's first ten years. But copper was found in great abundance. The Old Dominion Mine, located near the original Alice Gulch silver claims, was established in 1881 and continued to expand steadily. The town of Globe began to grow in leaps and bounds, with stately commercial buildings lining the main roadway, or Broad Street as it came to be known.

Buildings with thriving businesses and saloons lined Broad Street for five blocks, and new homes sprung up on the adjacent hillsides. Horses, stages, freightwagons and folks on foot rambled up and down this vital thoroughfare. There were continuous fires and floods that nearly destroyed the entire business district. But each time, these determined citizens came together to rebuild and continued to prosper. Some folks claim that Globe was just as wild and wooly as its counterpart Tombstone. Others believe North Broad Street was even more violent, with its vast number of murders, suicides, gunfights and lynchings.

By the end of the nineteenth century, Globe was one of the largest and busiest cities in Arizona. The railway came to town, which aided the mining industry and brought in more residents, and the town continued growing. The first twenty years of the 1900s was known as Globe's golden years. The Old Dominion Mine was in full operation, and two other copper mines began to operate in nearby Miami.

Soon after World War I, the Old Dominion Mine's quality began to decline. The ore grade fell, and profits were borderline. Water in the underground tunnels became a work hazard and increased production costs. The mine shut down in 1924 and was closed for good by 1931.

Life in Globe looked a bit dismal during the Great Depression. Men moved their families to find employment in other nearby towns. The copper mines in Miami slowed down or closed operations as well. Businesses were forced to shut down, making both cities resemble ghost towns.

The Second World War brought on demand for copper, and some of the old mines were reopened to meet the demands of war production. After the war, there were many productive years, despite the constant fear of recessions and strikes. The community continued to make its mark in the mining field for several more years.

So, why are Miami and Globe two of the most haunted towns in Arizona? In its early days, Globe was one of the wealthiest towns in the area. Men came to the town hoping to strike it rich and dwell in their wealth. Where there is wealth, there is also greed—and sometimes death. Occasionally, the less fortunate families became poor and unhappy with their lives and saw no way out; murder and suicide raged between despondent couples. Accidents were abundant, along with disease and epidemics. It was a hard life—and death came even harder.

I had visited Globe in the 1980s and 1990s, but it wasn't until I organized my paranormal team, MVD Ghostchasers, in 1994 that I developed an interest in the historic mining town. The team made several mini ghostly explorations to the hotels, restaurants and cemeteries before bringing up a small group of investigators to do a short walking tour of Broad Street and the Old Gila County Jail in 2003 under the guidance of local historian Kip Culver.

Amazed with the town's haunted history, I soon organized a larger group of interested paranormal investigators who wanted to spend the night in the old jail. Proudly, I can say we were the first paranormal group given permission to do an overnight investigation in 2006. Today, the Old Gila County Jail is one of the most popular locations in Globe where you just might encounter a ghost.

Globe is now known as one of the most haunted cities in Arizona, and several of its historic locations have appeared on various paranormal TV shows. Paranormal tours and investigations are abundant in the old mining town. You can attend one of several paranormal investigative events almost every weekend at one of many haunted buildings.

And don't forget, Globe comes alive every fall for the annual Ghosts of Globe Tour, where reenactors guide you through the dark alleys and streets, telling the stories of the spirits' explosive lives—and how they met their tragic deaths.

Disclaimer: While the majority of these ghostly tales are true and backed by researched documents, some of the stories have been handed down through the years and might simply be legend and folklore. Some of the tales come from the views and perspectives of enthusiastic historians, scholars, paranormal investigators and local citizens. Remarkably, they have all come together to share the wonderful tales of the ghosts of Globe.

1
GLOBE TRAIN DEPOT

The Gila County, Globe and Northern Railroad reached Globe, Arizona, in late 1898. In just a few months, a new passenger-freight depot stood along the tracks with the Globe business district nearby. It was originally built in the wood-frame style of many other early stations along the line. But in a very short time, it was one of the busiest locations in the booming town of Globe.

It was not long before that heavy rail traffic needed separate freight and passenger depots. A new freight depot was built in 1909. The architectural firm of Trost and Trost was commissioned in the mid-1910s to design a new depot complex, and by mid-1916, the main building was completed. Within the next year, the railroad restaurant and a Wells Fargo office were built next to the new station.

The Globe Railroad Station and adjacent buildings were built of fired red brick with concrete embellishments, elaborate cornices and multipaned windows. Offices of the division engineer, dispatcher and superintendent occupied the second floor of the station. The first level housed the ticket office, waiting rooms, baggage area and telegrapher's office.

After World War II, passenger service dwindled, and the passenger train made its final run from Globe on December 31, 1953. The building has been used by several businesses and organizations over the years.

Welcome to Globe—rear entrance to the 1916 Globe Train Depot. *Author's collection.*

THE FATE OF MARY DANIELS

Mary C. Daniels, a housewife of Globe, was on her way to witness the departure of the men from Gila County who had been drafted into the service during World War I. It was speculated the thirty-five-year-old woman, originally from England, stepped in front of the freight train from a point where she was unable to see it approaching on that early April 26, 1918 evening. The first car knocked her to the track and ran over her body. Before the train could be halted, two more cars had run over her. When her body was rescued from under the wheels, it was found that both of her legs had been severed above the knees. Dr. Wightman arrived shortly after the accident to render first aid before Daniels was taken to the county hospital. She never regained consciousness and died.

Daniels and her husband shared an eight-year-old daughter named Francis. Her funeral services were held at 5:00 p.m. at St. John's Episcopal Church in Globe. Pastor F.M. Johnson led the services with interment at the Globe Cemetery.

Young Frances was left without a parent and is one of the sad features of this haunting tragedy. Mary's husband was serving on the front in the Great War in France with an English regiment. At the time of the accident, he was in Sussex, England, with the Canadian engineers, awaiting orders for duty in France. He was notified of his wife's accident by a cablegram. Mrs. George Evans cared for Frances until word was received from the grieving father.

No other information about the cause of the accident was learned. Members of the train crew were unable to account for Daniels's failure to hear the approaching train, unless the wind (which was blowing at the time) carried the sound away from her. When Mary stepped across the track, the cars were so close that it was impossible to stop the train in time to prevent hitting her.

RAILWAY CLERK KILLS SELF BY POISON

Frederick Stanley Mattey, a thirty-five-year-old man, was the supply clerk for the Arizona Eastern Railroad in Globe. He died by suicide on September 24, 1924, by taking poison early one afternoon in the warehouse adjoining his office.

Mattey had arrived from Hutchinson, Kansas, just two weeks earlier with his wife, Mabel, and two small daughters. He was absent from work the day before his demise, complaining of a slight illness. The following day, he arrived at the office at 7:30 in the morning, thirty minutes earlier than usual, and appeared to be in his normal frame of mind, according to his associates.

Shortly after 8:00 a.m., Mattey was seen at the desk of one of the stenographers, where he was engaged in writing some letters. Two letters telling of his contemplated suicide were later found on his person. One was addressed to his wife, with whom he was apparently on the best of terms, and the other was addressed to C.R.Y. Hind, the manager of the Old Dominion Bank at Globe. Financial affairs were thought to be the reason for the despondency that caused his destruction. The full text of the letters was divulged by the railroad officials.

A stairway in the Globe Train Depot. *Author's collection.*

After finishing the letter writing, Mattey was seen entering the warehouse with a ledger under his arm, and it was thought that he had gone there to do some paperwork. Sometime later, Mr. Devlin, the son of Frank Devlin, a storekeeper, discovered the lifeless body of Mr. Mattey. The sheriff's office was notified, and Chief Deputy

Walter Nearlen visited the scene, accompanied by the coroner. Dr. R.D. Kennedy was called, and upon investigation of the manner of death and after finding the letters, it was decided that an inquest was not necessary. The body of Mattey was removed to the Jones Funeral Home and was buried in the Globe Cemetery.

Little was known of the deceased, other than that he had been a railroad clerk in Hutchinson, Kansas, before coming to Globe, where he resided on North Third Street.

E.F. Breyer Is Killed at Globe

Emil F. Breyer, the manager of the Globe Theater, was killed in an accident at 10:00 in the morning on November 18, 1919. The accident occurred near the freight depot in Globe. At the time, Breyer, with two or three other men, was engaged in unloading a carload of automobiles. One auto had been taken from the car, and the second was still suspended with the front end about five feet in the air. Breyer stooped under it and leaned over to pick up some blocking that had held the first car in place. At the moment he stooped over, the chain that was holding up the front end of the second auto broke, and the vehicle crashed down on him. In the shipping of automobiles, the front wheels are generally removed, and this fact allowed the auto to strike Breyer on the head. His skull was crushed, and death came almost instantaneously.

Emil F. Breyer was about thirty-five years old. He was married and left behind a wife and child. Mrs. Breyer had left Globe to go to Missouri, where she was summoned on account of the sickness of a relative. Breyer was buried in the Globe Cemetery.

The Murder of Bischofshausen

Bertha Bischofshausen, angry because her young son Bruce was to be taken from her life, spent time in the Gila County Jail while her soon to be late ex-husband, Curt R. Bischofshausen, suffered in the county hospital at the point of death, a bullet imbedded in his spine. Bertha Bischofshausen allegedly fired a pistol at him, claiming self-defense.

The front entrance of the 1916 Globe Train Depot. *Author's collection.*

The shooting occurred in a Pullman sleeper car, berth no. 7 on the *Apache Unlimited*, at 8:30 p.m. The man and a young boy had just boarded the train in order to transport the child to Texas on a superior court order.

After a long pattern of misconduct by Bertha, compounded by a recent divorce, the courts appointed Curt as the responsible parent of Bruce.

Now, Bertha Bischofshausen could be seen alone on a cot in the jail, dry-eyed with traces of tear stains on her cheeks from a hysterical and sleepless night of pacing the floor in her cell. Bertha had been arrested on the platform at the Globe Train Depot and surrendered a .32-caliber pistol.

The troubles began when welder Curt Bischofshausen returned home from a business trip and found his unfaithful wife in bed with another gentleman at a nearby hotel. An article in the *Arizona Silver Belt* from March 28, 1923, states, "The case is an echo of recent proceedings in the police court in which Mrs. Bischofshausen was arrested in company with Pete Harrison, a restaurant man, on charges of violating the city ordinances in Globe."

Bertha was fined $250 for lewd acts. That was the straw that broke Curt Bischofshausen's back, so to speak. He declared the marriage was over, filed for a divorce and made arrangements with his family in Texas to properly raise his young son.

His angry wife was not going to make this transition easy. Bertha and her friend Hazel Tinney, a waitress at the Dominion Hotel, drove to Miami, looking to purchase a gun. Their first stop was at the local hardware store, but the cost of a new pistol was way above Bertha's price range. The women headed into a secondhand store, where Bertha purchased a used .32-caliber pistol for fifteen dollars. Hazel Tinney bought shells for Bertha's weapon, telling the clerk they were going to hunt for rabbits.

After securing the gun, the ladies headed back to Globe. Bertha desperately searched for her ex-husband and three-year-old child. Someone informed her that Curt was leaving on the next train to Texas. Filled with anger, she dashed to the train depot and made her way to the steps of the Pullman car.

She boarded the train, telling the conductor it was her right as a mother to see her young son off. Curt and young Bruce were lying on a berth in the Pullman car. Bertha entered the car, gun in hand. Curt rose to his feet, and a tug of war ensued. Nobody ever knew whose hands were on the weapon and who actually fired the gun, but Curt Bischofshausen was shot in the abdomen during the struggle, a bullet lodging in his spine. He was rushed to the county hospital but died at 6:15 a.m. the following morning on March 29, 1922. Bertha was immediately arrested and locked in a jail cell. There she sat for days until she was released on a $10,000 bail bond.

Curt's father, a German immigrant residing in Sweetwater, Texas, traveled by train to Globe to retrieve his son's body and escort it back to Haskell, Texas, where he was buried. One could feel his sorrow as he waited for the train to take them home

Bertha's trial was held several months later. Being the only surviving parent, she regained custody of her son. The courtroom was filled to capacity the day of her trial. Women gathered and begged for the woman's freedom. They believed Curt had been abusive and that Bertha had only acted in self-defense.

Bischofshausen's German father once again made the long trip by train. He sat alone in the courtroom, hoping for a fair trial and justice for his son. Things did not go according to plan; surprisingly, the jury and judge acquitted Bertha Bischofshausen, and she was set free. There seemed to be no proof who fired the gun. The secondhand weapon was not in great shape, and it was declared that it was fired by accident. Curt's father was outraged and had to be contained. There was nothing more he could do, so he spent several more hours at the depot waiting for his train ride back to Sweetwater.

One would like to think Bertha turned her world around and lived a long and happy life—but it wasn't meant to be. She remarried, raised her son and eventually moved to California, where she committed several petty crimes, ended up in San Quentin Prison and later died at an asylum.

At a recent overnight stay at the Globe Train Depot, Debe Branning, Colleen Sulzer, Chance Houston, Carolee Jackson and Fallon Franzen had full access to the facility for an exclusive investigation. After conducting a lengthy EVP session upstairs, the group had come back down to refresh and review their data before starting another session in yet another area of the depot. Standing in a stairwell by the rear door to the train platform, Carolee began to hear a gentleman speaking German. Having taken a German language class in school, she recognized the distinct accent but wasn't able to make out the words. Some people believe this voice could be the residual energy from the elder Mr. Bischofshausen. Does his grief and anger remain within the walls of the old train depot? Listen closely: "Ruhe in Frieden."

THE SPIRITS OF JOHN AND LOLA WILLIAMS

The old railroad yards in Globe, Arizona, were once the scene of an attempted murder and suicide. On October 5, 1909, the body of John Williams was found near the railroad turntable. What led up to that fatal night had been brewing for some time.

For several months, Williams and his wife had not been on good terms. Mrs. Williams had been working for a Mrs. Sutton as a domestic. It was said by those who knew the family that it was because of her husband's suspicion that she would not give him her earnings that the troubles arose.

As the marital tension increased, more heated arguments ensued between the couple. During one argument, Mr. Williams broke a chair across his wife's body. Mrs. Williams swore out a warrant for her husband's arrest. A short time later, she filed for divorce, alleging cruelty and failure to provide.

Williams made several attempts to gain a reconciliation, but without avail; his inability to live on his wife's earnings rankled in his breast. He grew morbid. What must have the degree of frustration been for a fit of insanity to overcome him? His brutal attempt to murder his wife soon followed.

Mrs. Williams had been visiting the downtown district with Mrs. Phillips in whose house she had lived since the separation from her husband. The women were walking toward home around 10:30 p.m. As they were passing the Old Dominion warehouse, Williams stepped out from the shadows and confronted the frightened women. Without a word, he drew a revolver and fired two shots in quick succession at point-blank range. The first shot struck Mrs. Williams's body, directly over the heart. As the bullet hit her, she sank to the ground, screaming, "I'm shot!"

The second shot went wild. Mrs. Philips begged Williams not to shoot again.

"Keep quiet, or I will shoot you, too," he threatened.

Williams examined his revolver and ordered, "Stay here. I will be back in a minute." He then ran up Broad Street toward the railroad shops and disappeared.

Fortunately, Mrs. Williams owed her life to the fact that she was carrying a bottle of beer when her husband performed his most fiendish attempt to murder her. The bullet apparently struck the beer bottle. The bullet's impact with the glass deflected its deadly course. It entered her left breast, passed toward the right along her ribs, deflected off the bottle and became lodged in her left breast. The wound was not considered fatal.

A shattered beer bottle was found next to Mrs. Williams's body when she was picked up. Nothing was thought of the fact at the time, but from the course taken by the bullet, it became apparent that the interception of the bullet by the beer bottle had saved the woman's life. It was first thought that her injuries were deadly. But later, after she was taken to the county hospital and revived, the doctor stated that the wound might not prove fatal.

Witnesses said they saw Williams run south on Broad Street after the shooting and disappear. The entire police force of the city and county officers scoured the surrounding area for several hours in an attempt to capture the would-be murderer. The search was fruitless, but the large posse vowed not to give up.

The officers searched for Williams until the early hours of the morning, but the man was not found. His body was not located until the following morning. A group of his friends had gone out to search for him after daylight. They found his lifeless body in the railroad yards near the turntable, a bullet wound to the head, just behind his right ear, told the story of his death. Williams had only run a few hundred feet from the spot where he shot his wife when the realization of his deed became so overwhelming that he turned his revolver on himself.

An inquest was held over the remains of John Williams. A verdict of death by a bullet wound inflicted with suicidal intent was declared by the jury. Williams's body was buried later that day.

Two notes left by the dead man showed he wanted to murder his wife because he thought she had stopped loving him. After he shot her, he feared the gallows, since he truly believed he had killed her.

Sadly, Lola Jane Williams later died on January 23, 1920, at the county hospital from the effects of her injuries from the past October. Although her external wounds healed rapidly, the lesion on her lung became worse instead of better—the woman gradually wasted away. She was little more than a skeleton when she died.

The ghost of Williams might still be roaming the remains of the old railroad yard in Globe. Gunshots and the sound of shattering glass in the late-night air could be a sign of the lost lover's last act.

Several years ago, Debe Branning and Megan Taylor were walking on Broad Street near the old train depot. Megan stopped her pace and said, "Did you just see what I saw down by the railroad tracks?"

Debe admitted she saw someone walking, but it resembled more of a blur. "I just saw a man walking, or should I say, more like stumbling along the tracks. And then he fell to the ground and disappeared."

Could it have been the residual energy of John Williams when he went out of control, playing out those moments of insanity before he ended his life? It is well known that railroad tracks and waterways hold energy and can aid in the magnification of spirits. The Globe train depot has both of these elements—railroad tracks and Pinal Creek—at the rear of the building. Follow the tracks behind the Globe train depot and feel the sorrow, anguish and temper of those who had lost track of their emotions.

Haunted Globe train tracks. *Courtesy of Carolee Jackson.*

Rita Olsen of Arizona Ghost Adventure Tours has investigated the train depot with her investigative tour group several times. The group has heard a man speaking in German in the waiting room and has also recorded a female speaking on the upper floors of the depot. "Late one afternoon, we had finished setting up for the evening's event and decided to run out to get something to eat before the guests arrived," Rita noted. "We left a digital camera running while we were having dinner. Having finished early, we had time to play back the digital recorder and were surprised at what we heard. First, we were able to hear the door to the depot close. Then we began to hear footsteps on the tiled depot floor. The most amazing EVP we caught was as a woman's voice. She had a thick British accent and stated her name as 'Eleanor.'"

Justin Celani and his crew of investigators, Project Paranormal Arizona, spent the night investigating the train depot and smaller freight depot as well. "This location was beautiful but also had us feeling that people were walking around on the second floor. We would be sitting on a couch in one of the rooms and could hear what sounded like someone walking down the (wooden floor) hallway and the clang of metal. Another moment later, two of the members felt something touch them—one right after the other. Later, we went over to the smaller depot next to the main train station. We were doing lights-out, and I saw a figure walk across the outside of the window as if a person was passing by in the distance. The team went outside to check out who it could be—there was no one walking anywhere near the buildings."

On a visit to Globe, Debe Branning, Carolee Jackson, Fallon Franzen, Chance Houston and Coleen Sulzer were fortunate to spend the night in the old historic depot. Molly Cornwall and Tom Thompson greeted Debe and handed her a set of keys that opened a variety of doors to the building and adjacent "baby depot." "Which one opens the front door?" Debe asked.

"Why, the very last one you try!" Tom joked.

About that same time, the clasp of a necklace Molly was wearing came lose, and the jewelry fell to the floor. "That was a gift from Kip," she smiled. "This necklace has a very secure closure, and it never comes loose unless Kip's spirit is around. I think it is his way of saying 'hello,' and he is happy you are here."

Later, they gathered to do an EVP session upstairs in Kip Culver's old office, still decked out like it was the day he passed. Debe and Colleen faced the desk and a closed glass window. Shortly after the session began, both women noted the shadow of a tall, slender man as he walked outside past the second-story window. But how could that be? Neither woman could believe their eyes and hoped it was caught on camera; unfortunately, it did not repeat itself.

The group went downstairs to the main floor near the ticket office and the staircase leading up to the second floor. It was the early hours of the morning, around 2:30 a.m., when they crawled into sleeping bags on air mattresses. Then the footsteps began walking in the hallway, accompanied by a knock here and there. But the oddest activity were the voices of a man and woman chatting on the second floor, directly at the top of the staircase. The conversation was muffled, almost like listening to a static radio. They could not interpret the words in the message, and it lasted for about twenty to thirty minutes.

In October 2019, Debe Branning and Cindy Lee were hosting a special Día de los Muertos doll painting class with about twenty guests attending in the lobby of the train depot. While the ladies painted, Cindy entertained them with the history of Día de los Muertos. She then offered a few giggles by reciting a number of silly Halloween jokes and riddles. She presented her final riddle to the group, but to her dismay, no one could come up with the correct answer. Silence filled the vast lobby. Suddenly, a man's disembodied voice was heard from the area of the baggage room and broke the silence with the correct answer to the riddle. "Did you hear that, too?" she motioned to the direction of the sound. "I did!" Debe nodded, "and I know the voice. That was Kip Culver!"

Always a prankster and a fan of a good joke, the spirited historian decided to play along while Cindy attempted to stump the guests.

Globe Train Depot
230 South Broad Street
Globe, AZ 85501

2
Law and Order

The Hanging Tree

As Globe grew and became a prosperous mining town in the 1880s, it was forced to remain dependent on supplies brought in by stagecoach and pack mule trains. Provisions and goods were carried by train to Casa Grande on the Southern Pacific Railroad. From there, they were loaded onto an eastbound stage for Pioneer Pass through the rugged Pinal Mountains. Next, they were taken by a mule train manned by a packer and a mounted Wells Fargo shotgun messenger for the remaining twelve miles to Globe.

On August 20, 1882, the men escorting the mule train were Frank Porter and Andy Hall. Along with the supplies they were packing was a strongbox loaded with $5,000 in gold coins along with the payroll for the McMorris Silver Mine.

Globe photographer Cicero Grimes, his brother Lafayette Grimes and an acquaintance, Curtis B. Hawley, heard about the payroll shipment coming on the stagecoach and made a plan to steal it after the transfer to the mule train. Their idea was to ambush the mule train and make it look like an "Indian scare," shooting off rifles and hoping Porter and Hall would run for cover without taking the gold and payroll with them.

At the Pioneer Pass stage station, Cicero Grimes watched Porter and Hall transfer the precious cargo onto the mule train and saddle the lead roan with the strongbox. Grimes was able to relay the information to his brother Lafayette and partner Curtis Hawley, who set up an ambush about four miles from Globe. Cicero returned to Globe, leaving the other men to carry out the deed.

At the scene of the ambush, Grimes and Hawley shot and killed the lead roan and grazed Andy Hall in the hip. Hall and Porter, now in great danger, retreated to take cover in the rocks and brush. The mules scattered in all directions as Hall instructed Porter to ride to Globe and get help—fast!

Meanwhile, Grimes had opened up the strongbox and emptied the gold coins into saddlebags. The plan seemed to be a success, and the two outlaws headed west on foot.

Mine owner Dr. William F. Vail of Globe happened to be out that morning, checking on his mining property and riding up the pass to do some fishing. You might say he was in the wrong place at the wrong time. Hearing the earlier shots fired, Vail rode off in an effort to escape any awaiting conflict. About a mile or so later, Vail encountered Grimes and Hawley. Their conversation made him suspicious, and he turned to ride away. The brutal outlaws shot him and left him for dead.

Meanwhile, a wounded Andrew Hall was able to corral some of the mules and set off to Globe on foot. He eventually reached the outlaws' hideout. Grimes fired a shot at Hall, later claiming he had mistaken him for an attacking Apache. The three men, Hall, Grimes and Hawley, began to walk side by side until Hall recognized the saddle bags as the Wells Fargo property. Hawley shot Hall in the back, and he fell to the ground. The bandits shot Hall seven more times.

Porter arrived back in Globe about noon and reported the attack. Immediately, a posse was formed, and the lawmen rode back to the ambush site. There, they found the dead men and the empty strongbox. Fortunately, Grimes and Hawley were tracked down, and sometime between 7:30 and 8:00 p.m., the sheriff and posse brought in from the Bloody Tanks took charge of the two prisoners and at once placed them in the jail. As soon as it became known that the murderers were in town, a large meeting took place at the jail, and after much discussion among the officers and the people, the prisoners were surrounded and taken to Stella's Hall, where an inquest court was organized and a full hearing was immediately held.

Lafayette Grimes and Curtis Hawley were charged as the murderers, although Cicero was engaged in the plot. Lafayette Grimes confessed and exonerated his brother. Grimes and Hawley forfeited their lives in a summary manner by their own confession made without intimidation.

It was decided to hang the two men without delay. The prisoners asked for three hours' time and promised to reveal the stolen money's hiding place. This arrangement was excepted, and they, in the company of about thirty citizens, headed to the foothills of the Pinal Mountains, about four miles from town. There, they pointed out the hiding places of the money. Most of it was found and taken in charge by the agent of the express company.

The group of men returned to the hall when Hawley asked for time to make out a written confession and arrange his worldly affairs. This, too, was granted, and at a quarter before 2:00 a.m., the church bell was heard to toll. A procession was formed, the prisoners guarded on either side by well-armed men as they moved in the direction of a large sycamore tree on Main Street (now Broad Street) near Pinal Creek.

It was 2:00 in the morning of August 24, 1882. All was quiet and orderly, not a word was spoken nor a whisper heard as the solemn march of death advanced. Globe townspeople marched the two men, John Hawley and Lafayette Grimes, "out the door of Stallo's Hall, nooses placed around their necks. At last, the ropes were tossed over the limb of a huge old sycamore that stood in the middle of Main Street. The townspeople tugged at the ropes and sent John Hawley and Lafayette Grimes to oblivion—both fastened to the same limb of the hanging tree."

The hanging tree on Broad Street. *Courtesy of Bullion Plaza Cultural Center.*

The Hanging Tree Historic Marker. *Author's collection.*

All of the businesses, including saloons, closed their doors early in the evening. No disorder occurred, and not a single drunken man was seen on the streets.

This ended the terrible scene of retributive justice to these hardened criminals. Cicero Grimes confessed to participating in the crime, but owing to the fact that he was not on the scene when the action was committed, he was sent back to jail to await further action. His poor, sickly wife and four small children made a scene to draw sympathy from the crowd.

The dead men were left hanging to the tree until 8:00 a.m., when an inquest was held by the coroner and the bodies were handed over to the sheriff.

The victims of the executed murderers (Hall and Vail) were buried Monday afternoon at 2:00 p.m. by the Methodist church. After an eloquent and touching sermon by Mr. Calfee, the bodies were followed to their final resting places by a large number of citizens and families.

A fire on June 9, 1894, wiped out many businesses, including the old sycamore tree. Two years later, the sheriff declared the hanging tree to be a public hazard and hired a local cowboy to chop it down.

The original Globe Hanging Tree is long gone, but a sycamore sapling is growing near the bridge at Pinal Creek, and a monument that was placed in 1997 describes that dark day in Globe history.

The *Arizona Daily Star* said the hanging was "a monument to the sturdy spirit of justice." Does the residual energy of the men who met their fates on the hanging tree still suspend over the area?

Globe Hanging Tree (Marker)
Broad Street, 0.1 mile south of Hackney Avenue
Globe, AZ 85501

SARAH SORIN: A GHOST ABOVE THE LAW

The Amster building stands as one of Globe's best-preserved structures and shares its history with some of the city's finest buildings.

Nathan Amster arrived in Globe in 1896, about one year after he had immigrated to the United States from his homeland of Romania. His main pursuit in Globe was mining, especially after he bonded the Continental Mine west of Globe. He also had an interest in the railroads and promoted rail lines to the Copper Hill vicinity.

The enterprising Amster eventually began investing in downtown Globe property and helped fund the construction of the Amster building in 1909. The Amster building design is, in the vernacular, of the Georgian revival style. Its fired red bricks were highlighted by a decorative stepped parapet, cast metal cornices and pilasters complete with dentils and brackets. These days, the building offers a more modern look, as some of the original design has been altered.

An eating and drinking establishment called the Lodge was one of the building's early tenants. It was a popular place for the citizens of Globe to dine. Later, Wightman's Drug Store highlighted the lower level of the building along Broad Street. From that time on, there was always a drugstore business at that location, where citizens could fill their prescriptions, shop for personal products and even purchase small gifts. The basement was home to a newspaper office and a church. The second floor has been used for professional law offices—a convenient location with the former Gila County Courthouse just across the street. It is also the home of one of the more famous ghosts of Globe, that of Sarah Herring Sorin. Known as the first female lawyer in Arizona, Sorin was also the first female lawyer from Arizona admitted to practice law before the U.S. Supreme Court in April 1906.

Sarah Sorin was born in New York City on January 15, 1861. She was educated in New York and moved to Arizona to be with her family in 1882. She began her career teaching elementary school, becoming the first female teacher in Tombstone, Arizona. She studied law under the guidance of her father, Attorney William Herring. In 1892, she was permitted to practice law in Arizona. Sarah returned to New York in 1893 to attend the New York University Law School and completed her coursework in May 1894. She returned to Tombstone in June 1894. She and her father became partners in a Tombstone law firm. Colonel Herring and Sarah Sorin decided to relocate their law practice to the growing city of Tucson, later calling it Herring and Sorin.

The spirit of Sara Sorlin is seen at the Amster building. *Author's collection.*

Sarah married Thomas Sorin in July 1898. Sorin was a rancher, mineralogist and a journalist for the famous *Tombstone Epitaph*. They lived on his ranch near Tombstone for many years. Sorin was often away from home with his business, so Sarah eventually moved back to the family home in Tucson in 1902. There, she became more involved in the family law firm.

After her father died, Sarah moved her practice to Globe, where she became the attorney for the Old Dominion Copper Company and specialized in mining law. The tall, slender lawyer was well liked by the citizens of Globe.

Unfortunately, Sarah Herring Sorin became ill with influenza and died of pneumonia in Globe, Arizona, on April 30, 1914, at the age of fifty-three. She was buried in Evergreen Memorial Park in Tucson, Arizona. But some Globe residents believe her ghost still roams her old law office above the Palace Pharmacy.

Debe Branning was with a group of friends who had traveled up to Globe for the Annual Ghosts of Globe Tour. The group dressed in colorful Halloween costumes and gathered in a tour group near the old Amster building. After listening to the dearly departed reenactor on the corner, they prepared to walk to their next stop. Cindy Lee suddenly looked up and pointed to a window on the second floor of the building. "I just saw a fair-haired lady looking down from the window at us!" Cindy smiled. "Then she faded away."

Various employees have witnessed a woman with light hair wearing a long, dark skirt and white ruffled blouse on the upper floors of the Amster building. Her image has been seen standing behind patrons as they glance into the mirrors in the restrooms. Employees have come to work in the mornings to find all of the lights turned on in the building. Some workers have been so disturbed by the beautiful specter that they refused to return to work. Attorney Tom Thompson occupies the same office space that Sarah did on the second floor. He noted that it is hard to keep steady staff on the job due to the strange activity.

Other witnesses have seen a woman in a white blouse looking from the second story windows and gazing over at the old Gila County Courthouse building. Is it the spirit of Sara Herring Sorin planning her strategy for a judgment day in court? Or is she studying the law of reincarnation: If there is anything unresolved or incomplete at the end of your lifetime, is your soul allowed an opportunity to return in human form to resolve or complete it? You be the judge.

Amster Building (currently a CVS Pharmacy)
100 North Broad Street
Globe, AZ 85501

GILA COUNTY COURTHOUSE

The early offices for Gila County were located in simple adobe buildings on the corner of Broad and Oak Streets. In time, the county purchased the simple adobe buildings, and in 1887, they were torn down and demolished to make room for a two-story courthouse and jail. Unfortunately, the new structure was too small to properly serve the community from the start. Proposals to increase the size of the building were made, but a lack of finances delayed any changes until after the turn of the twentieth century.

By 1905, the economy in the area had greatly improved. Gila County was authorized to issue bonds in the sum of $40,000 to construct a brand-new courthouse. Architect William R. Norton designed the stately building, and Peter Wilson won the bid for its construction.

Gila County rented temporary quarters for their offices while the original two-story courthouse was torn down. The dacite stones were salvaged and reused in the grand new building. Work began in 1906, and the construction was completed in March 1907.

This magnificent new building drew in great reviews from the townspeople of Globe. The design was called modern composite, having Egyptian ornamentation and a French Renaissance roof arrangement. Its interior features included decorative pilasters, arches, fireproof vaults and high ceilings. A beautiful grand staircase with copper-clad railings nearly filled a central atrium. Balconies were designed to look down on the stairway. Light came from a skylight high above the stairs.

The new building had space for all of Gila County's functions. The sheriff's office and a sixteen-cell jail occupied the ground floor/basement level. Above this were the offices of the assessor, recorder clerk and probate judge, along with the county supervisors' meeting chambers. The courtroom was placed in the upper level and included the judge and jury chambers, the offices of the district attorney and a law library.

All seemed to move along smoothly until the jail began to overflow. A new jail was built behind the alleyway of the courthouse in 1909. Four years later, the interior of the courthouse was remodeled at a grand total of

The Gila County Courthouse in 1912. *Courtesy of Molly Cornwell.*

$12,000. Over the years, many interior modifications were made, including the addition of a much-needed elevator in 2015. Some of the windows were infilled with matching dacite blocks.

For over seventy-five years, the county business of Gila County was carried out in the majestic 1906 courthouse. But eventually, even this building became overcrowded and outdated. The county functions were moved down the road to a more modern facility in southwest Globe in 1978. Fortunately, in 1984, the building became the home for the Cobre Valley Center for the Arts. The building became part of a long-range restoration plan that continues today. The Gila County Courthouse was placed in the National Register of Historic Places in 1975.

Debe Branning and Megan Taylor decided to drive up to Globe and explore the historic courthouse one cloudy afternoon in the early spring. It was a quiet day, and there were no other visitors at the arts center. The woman at the front desk encouraged them to walk around and enjoy the many quilts and art displays presented throughout the building. "Don't forget to check out the courtroom," she noted. "The former courtroom is now a fabulous stage and playhouse for our local thespians! We have another production coming up very soon!"

The two ladies went upstairs to the third floor and gazed into the grand courtroom/theater. One could almost feel the energy that filled the room, with tense crimes of theft, murder and shootings and other high-profile cases of the day. Walking out of the courtroom, the girls noted a doorway to the right of them that was left open just a crack. They slowly opened the door to find a storage room full of theater costumes and props.

"Wow! Just look at all of this cool stuff!" Megan gazed around the room.

Suddenly, a voice of a little girl giggled inside the room.

"Did you hear that?" Debe asked.

"I sure did!" Megan responded. "Little girl, you don't have to hide. Come out and see us. We won't hurt you."

"I have candy," Debe pulled a piece of wrapped candy from her purse. "I'll place it here on the chair, and you are welcome to take it."

Around that time, the ladies could hear someone coming up the grand staircase, and they decided to leave the prop room—after all, they probably shouldn't have been in there in the first place.

"Are you girls alright?" the docent asked. "I thought I heard somebody scream up here. Did one of you get hurt?"

"We are both fine," Megan assured her. "We are just exploring this fabulous building."

The Majestic Gila County Courthouse. *Courtesy of Rita Olsen.*

Megan and the docent became engaged in conversation, which gave Debe a chance to head down the grand staircase on her own. Having reached the main floor, she turned right and started down a hallway that housed several art studios. Suddenly, an unseen entity ran past her into one of the rooms. She looked around and remembered there was nobody else in the building. Debe turned around and slowly headed in the direction of the staircase near the front door. Megan and the docent descended the steps around that same time.

"Something rushed past us as we came down the stairs," Megan informed her.

"And then whomever it was ran down this hallway and into that room!" Debe pointed.

They could feel that the docent was getting a little uncomfortable, and it was time to go.

Years later, they learned that the assailant of a prisoner, Kingsley Olds, had hidden in the courthouse after hours and made his escape out of the building the following day, completely undetected. The man who murdered Kingsley Olds fired a shot from a courthouse window into the open bars of the man's jail cell. Does the spirit of the unknown sharpshooter still lurk in

The Gila County Courthouse at night. *From Wikimedia.*

the protective walls of this massive fortress? And who is the little girl hiding in the upstairs prop room? The show must go on, and from what we have learned here, it plays out quite often.

Gila County Courthouse
(also known as the Cobre Valley Center for the Arts)
101 North Broad Street
Globe, AZ 85501

THE BRIDGE OF SIGHS

Like New York and Venice, Globe has its own Bridge of Sighs. It leads from the old Gila County Jail to the former Gila County Courthouse and was the passageway over which the prisoners condemned to death in the courtroom were escorted as they made their way to the condemned cell before being led to the gallows below. The bridge is made of steel and connects the second story of the jail to the second floor of the courthouse.

An eerie-looking catwalk spans a gloomy back alley, holding on to the moments of fear and despair from those prisoners whose boots echoed with each step they took along the steel grids hovering over the brick passageway. There have been speculations about murders and hangings taking place in the towering steel structure in the past. Paranormal investigators have uncovered the true reasons a ghostly presence is felt in the darkened alley between the two historic buildings.

On May 2, 1912, a Globe prisoner died by suicide after jumping off the runway to the ground below, where he instantly died. Frank Ballant, fearing the sentence he was about to receive in the superior court for murderous assault, told fellow inmates that he would rather be dead than serve a long term in the state penitentiary in Florence, Arizona. He had recently been convicted of assault with intent to commit murder against a Mexican man in Miami in March 1912.

While crossing the Bridge of Sighs, Ballant, age twenty-nine, suddenly stopped in the middle of the passageway and made a sensational leap over the railway, dropping forty feet to the ground below—his brains mashing on the hard pavement. This act bewildered his captors, and the story made headlines in local newspapers.

Ballant, an Italian miner, was visited in his cell by an unknown man who convinced him that he would get a ninety-nine-year sentence in prison, as he had committed a crime of the first degree. He was found guilty by a jury in the superior court of intent to murder with a deadly weapon.

Men have jumped from the eerie Bridge of Sighs. *Author's collection.*

After the disturbing visit, Ballant brooded in his cell and became very depressed, talking constantly about the case. He gave away his tobacco before leaving the jail, stating that he had no further use for it. Had Ballant waited and taken his sentence, he would have discovered that a light sentence had been issued to him.

The unusual spectacle was witnessed by several prisoners confined in the county jail, and they were summoned to testify before a coroner's jury. Ballant was a native of Cosenza, Italy, and left relatives in the United States and Italy. He had lived in Globe for about eight years.

Frank Ballant's unsettled spirit has been sentenced to roam the Bridge of Sighs and eerie alleyway in Globe for all eternity during reenactment performances for various history events. But many people have seen shadows on the Bridge of Sighs and images of a man looking over the railway. Paranormal investigators have recorded EVPs of screams and a voice stating, "Let's end it here."

Debe Branning recalled the day several years ago when she discovered the story of Ballant's suicidal fall from the Bridge of Sighs in her early research of online newspapers. She immediately emailed Globe historian Kip Culver about the death of Ballant. Kip was always searching for Globe ghost tales to share with Debe but seemed a little puzzled with this one.

"Forty feet?" he questioned. "They have to be talking about someplace else—that can't be forty feet."

Debe insisted that was how the newspaper article read and sent him a copy. In little or no time, Kip was out in the alley with a yardstick, measuring the size of the stone brick on the courthouse. He then stood there counting the bricks that led up from the cobblestone alley to the foreboding Bridge of Sighs.

A couple hours later, Debe received an email.

"You were right!" Kip cheered! "Men have fallen to their death from the Bridge of Sighs!"

Ever since then, the tale of the Bridge of Sighs has been a mainstay for local paranormal investigations and the topic at all the Ghosts of Globe tours each Halloween.

The catwalk is located near the corner of Broad and Oak Streets, behind the old courthouse that is now the Cobre Center of the Arts Building.

Bridge of Sighs
177 East Oak Street
Globe, AZ 85501

THE 1910 GILA COUNTY JAIL

One of the first—and necessary—structures to be constructed in the early pioneer towns of the Old West was the town jail. The first jail in Gila County was a small, one-cell adobe building in Globe. The jail was moved to the basement of the new courthouse, which included the sheriff's office, in 1888. The adjacent exercise yard also contained the dreaded gallows, which were used when needed. When the larger courthouse was constructed in 1906, the jail and sheriff's office were placed side by side on the ground floor.

The booming mining town soon needed a much larger jail. In November 1909, a three-story structure constructed of reinforced poured concrete was conveniently located behind the courthouse. It was completed in 1910, and Sheriff John Henry Thompson and his deputies moved into the new facility, ready to maintain law and order in the rowdy town.

The jail's façade featured a cornice with dentils, quoins on the corners and fancy lintels over the window, the design blending in with that of the other downtown buildings. The first floor housed the new sheriff's office in front, and above this were several small cells for female and juvenile prisoners. The rear three-story section contained steel cell blocks. It is said the cells were moved to Globe from the recently closed Territorial Prison in Yuma.

The front entrance to the 1910 Gila County Jail. *Courtesy of Carolee Jackson.*

Jail cells in the old 1910 Gila County Jail. *Courtesy of Carolee Jackson.*

The jail closed in 1978, when a new, modern facility was opened a few miles away. By the early 1990s, the old jail was abandoned and falling into disrepair. Recognizing what a treasure the historic building could be to the community restoration began to make it a tourist attraction. Repairs were done, old photographs of sheriffs were hung back on the walls, newspaper clippings were gathered and law and order relics were put on display, leaving the graffiti intact on the cell walls. Soon, the jail was opened to the public for historic tours and special community events.

Although hundreds of men and women have been incarcerated within the dank walls of the old jail, the prisoner who is most talked about is a man by the name of Kingsley Olds.

Charged with assaulting and then drowning Lulu and Myrtle Goswick, aged eleven and twelve years, in the Salt River, Kingsley Olds was arrested and placed in the Gila County Jail on June 30, 1911, with his lower jaw shot away in an attempt, it was believed, to die by suicide after killing the two girls.

Olds rode into Globe and told a story of having been shot by a Native or Mexican, and it was feared that the girls had also been shot and killed.

Their bodies were found the next day in the water of the Salt River near Horseshoe Bend. They had been drowned. There was no sign of violence or assault. Their bodies were brought back to Globe by automobile.

A posse that had gone out to find the girls could find no corroboration of Olds's story. Only one trail of footsteps could be found, and they led to the spot where Olds's shotgun was found near the river. Olds's tongue was partly shot away, and he could not talk. He was supplied with paper and a pencil, and he wrote that he had gone bathing with the girls on a trip from the Goswick Ranch to the river. He said that while they were in the water, a Mexican took a shotgun from Olds's wagon and shot him. He then loss consciousness and had no idea what had happened to the girls.

Wesley Goswick, the father of the girls, was disarmed while coming to Globe, as he had the intention of killing Olds.

During Olds's stay in the jail's hospital cell, a nurse was assigned to sit outside the door and administer his medication. During an inquest interview the nurse was asked:

> *Question: He never said anything about death to you—or about the girls?*
>
> *Nurse: No, sir. The night before, he had been quieter than usual, and he told me he had seen the girls come to him, and he put his hand to his ear, and he said they were calling him and wanted him to come. I asked him if he wanted them to come to him, and he said, "Yes." I gave him morphine, and he was all right and sat up in bed and said that the girls would be back again after him. Next morning, he said the girls had been back again last night.*

Several years ago, Kip gave this author a very faint copy of a page of the inquest document that tells of Kingsley Olds seeing the ghosts of the girls in his cell right before he was murdered. How many cases are there of a ghost seeing ghosts?

On July 5, Olds was shot and instantly killed as he lay in the hospital cell in the Gila County Jail just before daylight. The shot was fired from a window in the judge's chambers, which overlooked Olds's cell. The murderer escaped, leaving their rifle behind. It was learned that they gained access to the chamber with keys stolen from the jailer's locker. It was found that they had punched a hole in the window screen and, resting their rifle barrel carefully on the window ledge, sent their first shot into Olds's right shoulder. It ranged downward through his right lung, and death was instantaneous.

The Gila County Jail and Courthouse in 1912. *Courtesy of Molly Cornwell.*

It has been rumored that the assailant walked out the main door of the courthouse at daylight and headed down Broad Street. Many residents recognized the shooter but turned their head in the other direction, using a bit of unauthorized frontier justice. It was also well known that Wesley Goswick was an avid hunter and a crack shot.

In January 2004, Debe Branning, the director of the MVD Ghostchasers, gained permission to hold the first overnight paranormal investigation of the Gila County Jail. It was a cold winter night—a very cold winter night—and guests filed into the jail, carrying sleeping bags, blankets, hats and coats. They loaded their paranormal equipment into the cell they selected for the night. A coveted space heater in the small entry office offered the only warmth, as the cold concrete walls promised no mercy.

The investigators broke up into small groups and explored every floor, including the third floor, where trustees were allowed to mingle near the infamous Bridge of Sighs. While reviewing data from that first investigation, there was (lost) footage of a ghostly prisoner standing on the Bridge of Sighs, an EVP of a gentleman greeting ("Hello, fellas") and a recording of a horrendous female scream near the women's cellblock. All in all, it was a very successful night. Kip Culver, the curator of the jail museum, sat in his then office throughout the evening to make sure the investigation was safe and secure. One by one, due to the cold air, the half-frozen ghost hunters packed up their bedrolls and equipment and called it a night. Soon, they were down to the last half-dozen investigators, who endured the chill until about 3:00 in the morning.

This started the trend of paranormal teams reserving and renting the jail for paranormal investigations, movie filming and other ghostly experiments. The MVD Ghostchasers have conducted several investigations at the old jail throughout the years, and it never disappoints.

In January 2018, Debe was back at the Gila County Jail, filming an episode of Travel Channel's *Ghost Adventures* ("Old Gila County Jail and Courthouse," 2018). It was an honor that she was asked to be the historian speaking about Kingsley Olds's cell and the girls' tragic deaths. The *Ghost Adventures* crew experienced a lot of activity that night, and it is an episode you don't want to miss.

Carolee Jackson of FOTOS (Friends of the Other Side) described some of her encounters with the ghosts at the old jail. "Where does one start with this building—from apparitions, voices/crying, footsteps, cell doors hanging open/shut, boxes or something large moving in the third-floor storage area—there is always something going on!"

Carolee continued to talk about some of the spirits she had communicated with at the jail over the years.

> *In November 2017, I met several in "spirit," although only a few offered a name and identifying life situations. Early on, I met "Benjamin" Whiting, a domestic violence charge followed with two-year sentence. Sandy blond hair going in every direction, steel-blue eyes. Came home very drunk, confronted by wife about alcohol and money and family responsibility. He lashed out, beating her severely, breaking the arm. He kept saying to me, "So sorry. Forgive me,"—remorseful.*
>
> *I met "Héctor" in the second-floor men's toilet, which is dense with the horrific energy of violence. Héctor was beaten and may have lost sight in one eye. Had the sense of not seeing what was coming from the left peripheral. Constantly blindsided, and men knew this weakness. I don't speak Spanish but heard "Hago daño," which I have since looked up, meaning "I hurt."*
>
> ["Evalina" in the women's cells] *was quick to get my attention and followed me for a bit. On the short side, very thin, long, stringy brown hair. What she relayed is that she was accused, lied about and sentenced one year for stealing money—money to feed her family, as her husband had fled long*

ago. Evalina ran away from her family as a teen, ending up with this man who brought her to Arizona. She kept asking, "Where is my boy? Is he okay?"

There was a man named Cassidy in cell 6—rude with offensive language. Very hostile and angry. This guy was incarcerated in the late '50s/early '60s by his appearance. Got an immediate headache from this meeting and left.

Cell 2 upstairs is where I met the lovely young Chinese woman who I called Jasmine due to the sweet aroma of the Jasmine flower with her presence. Jasmine is mixed-race, white and Chinese. She is about seventeen or eighteen years of age, very tiny in stature, long black hair, dark brown eyes. She was forced into prostitution at age twelve.

We met "Oswald" in the second-floor men's cell area during a dowsing rod session. Oswald, age twenty-eight, and his brother, perhaps age thirty, were caught in the act of stealing a horse. The brother got away, but Oswald did not.

Throughout the night, I heard audible voices not associated with the group in attendance with the paranormal investigation. I experienced a temperature drop into what I would call cold, energy shifting, movement detected, was touched and challenged.

Toward the last group EVP session, two male voices were being heard in the second-floor hall between the men's and women's areas. Several of us acknowledged the voices, and Debe suggested a couple of us go look. So, Robbin Jerich and I did just that. As soon as we got to the hall, the voices stopped, but our attention was drawn to the stairwell that took you up to the connecting bridge between the jail and courthouse. Robbin went up the stairs to the first landing and started to take pictures while we got a sense of the stairwell and energy within it. I was downstairs across from the open door. All of a sudden, loud as can be, we both heard a sigh right next to Robbin. Within seconds, I realized a large shadow was charging at me from the second window at the ladder on the floor. This shadow was huge. I couldn't move. The shadow went through me, leaving me icy cold—that was painful—and my breath came out in a cold fog. My energy was scattered a bit until I heard Robbin ask if I was okay. Honestly, I wasn't sure at first but then thought, "Holy crap! That was freaking amazing! How cool was that?" Robbin and I shared what we each saw and heard before joining the group again. It was then that we were told that the connecting bridge is called the Bridge of Sighs. I would not hesitate to revisit this jail in the future. Aside from the history, the personal experiences shared among us was pretty extensive for one night.

Right: The back stairway leading from the jail to the Bridge of Sighs. *Courtesy of Robbin Jerich.*

Below: The stairway leading up to the Bridge of Sighs. *Courtesy of Robbin Jerich.*

Rita Olsen, the current owner of Arizona Ghost Adventures, conducts frequent tours of the Gila County Jail. She offers evening investigations as well as overnight stays for guests who need to serve more time. Rita recalled an overnight tour during which one of the female guests selected to spend the night in the Kingsley Olds cell. It is an isolated area away from the large cell block. The investigator was lying on a cot covered with her sheet when it suddenly was pulled off her legs by some unseen force in the cell.

With an arsenal of paranormal equipment to borrow on her investigative tours, Rita invites her guests to explore the facility under her guidance. "The Old Gila County Jail is one of the most active sites in Globe," Olsen declared. "It is one of the most popular locations to do a paranormal investigation in Arizona."

Vincent "Vinny" Amico with Arizona Ghost Tours agrees. His team is another one of the current rotating investigative groups that offer exclusive paranormal investigations at the jail. "We have been coming to the historic jail since 2011," he stated. "After a while, the ghostly inmates have come to recognize us. When we hear that bang on the jail cell door, we know it is a greeting—their way of saying, "Hello."

The team has recorded many EVPs and enjoys using the latest paranormal equipment with guests to offer new investigative methods and experiments. Every investigative tour is different, and you never know which inmate you might interact with "in spirit."

If you are not in for an extended sentence, you can still attend a short-term, daytime tour of the jail on various weekends. You will be pardoned and paroled before dark—no nail file in a cake necessary.

Historic 1910 Gila County Jail
149 East Oak Street
Globe, AZ 85501

3

Native American Spirits

Besh-Ba-Gowah

Besh-Ba-Gowah is a two-hundred-room prehistoric Salado masonry pueblo located atop a broad ridge overlooking Pinal Creek. The site is set about one mile southwest of Globe and surrounded by a small city park and a museum with excavated items, including prehistoric pottery, stoneware and woven artifacts. The site is operated by the city as Besh-Ba-Gowah Archaeological Park and Museum.

Besh-Ba-Gowah was occupied by Salado populations between 1225 CE and 1400 CE. *Salado* is the term applied to the complex of cultural features of the prehistoric peoples who inhabited the Globe/Miami and Tonto Basin regions between 1150 CE and 1450 CE.

This pueblo consists of multistoried masonry room block clusters connected by long, narrow corridors or elongated plazas. These room blocks and corridors are situated around a large communal plaza area measuring twelve meters long (north–south) by twenty-seven meters wide (east–west).

The material recovered from Besh-Ba-Gowah has formed the foundation for our current understanding and definition of the Salado culture concept. Besh-Ba-Gowah is considered one of the Salado culture's type sites.

The all-walled architecture at Besh-Ba-Gowah was built with unshaped, large to moderately sized granite cobble masonry laid with a clay mortar. Evidence suggests that interior walls were commonly plastered with this mortar or a more

The Besh-Ba-Gowah ruins. *From Wikimedia.*

calcareous mixture, resulting in white-colored walls. There are some indications that at least selected exterior walls were also plastered with the original clay mortar. Often, the basal masonry course consisted of vertical slabs, presently considered characteristic of Salado masonry architecture.

Excavations at the Besh-Ba-Gowah site were funded originally by the Federal Emergency Relief Administration and then by the Work Projects Administration. The "ruin represents one of the few remaining, reconstructed and stabilized examples of archaeological projects undertaken within Arizona to alleviate critical unemployment during the Depression years."

Besh-Ba-Gowah was listed in the National Register of Historic Places in 1984.

The site was first surveyed and mapped in 1883 by Adolph Bandolier, and the ancient ruins that were occupied by both the Hohokam and Rio Salado Natives beginning in 1600 CE came to be known as Besh-Ba-Gowah. Some early excavation work was completed in the 1920s. Opportunely, in 1935, Irene Vickrey arrived at Besh-Ba-Gowah as the job supervisor of the excavation and performed her duties for the next five years. She proudly gave the site its name, which translates to "a place of metal" in Apache. Her team uncovered nearly 200 rooms and 350 burial sites. After her work was completed in 1940, the site was subsequently left unattended for nearly forty years.

In 1941, Vickrey involved Globe's community in bringing the city's ancient past to life by leading *Last Days of Besh-Ba-Gowah*, a grand pageant that was performed on the roof of the museum and climaxed in a reenactment of an attack by rival outsiders. The performance involved a small cast of adults and children. The night sky was lit up with colored lights, the high school provided music and the San Carlos Reservation Apache tribe performed a devil dance as the grand finale.

Irene Vickrey died in January 1946 at the age of thirty-five. She had come to Arizona with a respiratory problem, and working with the soil did not do any good for her health. She was buried in the Globe City Cemetery.

Louis Aguirre will be remembered and credited for his great efforts in completing the final preservation work on the ruins so that the historic site could be an educational asset for decades to come.

The many artifacts retrieved from Besh-Ba-Gowah when it was first excavated in the 1920s represent one of the largest single-site collections in existence. Today, the historical site is maintained with a small fund from the City of Globe and generous donations from supporters.

There are approximately 150 burial sites underneath the plaza; it is suspected that hereditary status was used. There were few rooms in the ruins that were accessed using ladders though roof hatchways. The current archaeological park at Besh-Ba-Gowah features prehistoric content in a number of reconstructed rooms. There are cross sections of the roof layered with mud, mats and reeds. The trail takes visitors to the ruins past the ceremonial room, where a quartz-covered sipapu full of turquoise dust was found. There are benches built into the room, an altar and four large posts supporting the roof. In addition, a small mound that appears to be a platform sits in this portion of the ruins.

In November 2017, the MVD Ghostchasers hosted a Globe Paranormal Workshop. One of the last stops before heading down to the Phoenix area was Besh-Ba-Gowah. Participant Carolee Jackson described some of the experiences she had that early autumn afternoon.

> *This was my second visit to the ruins, with* [paranormal] *experiences both times. The visit from this past weekend was definitely enhanced with the flute music Chance Houston played off his recording device and Colleen Sulzer's use of Native language.*

Chance played the recorded flute music while a few of us were in the three-story building. There was an older male in spirit that tucked himself into the corner behind Colleen. He tried not to be noticed, but good luck with that with us two ladies. Almost simultaneously, Colleen and I looked up to the second-floor access. Looking down was a woman in spirit, possibly late twenties in age, with three giggling children at her side. The children were full of curiosity but not quite brave enough to venture from the woman's side. The woman wanted me to relay to Chance, "Thank you for the music. A long time since hearing any." The heart chakra swelled with love and gratitude.

In a common area near the ceremonial room, the group gathered for a session utilizing the flute music again. About halfway into the session, I noticed several women in spirit among us, all ages, shifting their feet side to side and a few steps and back, repeatedly, slowly circling to the left. I found myself mimicking their movement and made myself stop so as not to contaminate anyone's audio. After Colleen asked questions in a Native language, there was a swell of acknowledgment and shock that the "white woman" spoke a dialect similar to theirs. I mentioned the women's shifting movement, to which Colleen stated it was probably a dance of theirs. The synergetic energy in our group complemented these women's, which may have been why they came forward. Very cool experience.

Opposite: Contacting ancient spirits in the Besh-Ba-Gowah ruins. *Author's collection.*

Above: Touring the Besh-Ba-Gowah ruins. *Courtesy of Carolee Jackson.*

Debe Branning recalled gathering the entire group to one area of the ruins so that they could feel the energy of the ancient spirits of Besh-Ba-Gowah together. Somewhere in the middle of the ceremony, it was almost like they were transported to another time and place. There was no sound, and the air became still. As Colleen continued chanting, calling out to the Native ancestors in their own tongue, a breeze filled the area where the group had assembled. It was as though all the plaza's spirits had encircled the paranormal visitors and were giving them a blessing. They were thankful the group had come that day to learn about their heritage and explore their traditions. A profound sense of peace and serenity was felt by everyone.

Besh-Ba-Gowah
1324 South Jesse Hayes Road
Globe, AZ 85501

BLOODY TANKS MASSACRE

The Bloody Tanks Wash was named after the Bloody Tanks Massacre of 1864, when Colonel King Woolsey and his men encountered a band of Apache warriors. A battle ensued, and the blood of the Apache was said to make the mountain stream run red.

Frontiersman King S. Woolsey was in the Arizona Territory in 1860 as a mule driver for the army, which also hired him as an Indian fighter. Woolsey made his way to the Miami area, where he entered a contract with the army to supply its animals with hay. In 1864, the army received a report that the Apache were in the Prescott area, stealing horses, cattle and food from the nearby ranchers—and there were a few murders committed as well.

Woolsey was put in charge of army volunteers and followed the trail of the Apache from the Prescott area to the junction of the Salt and Verde Rivers, then over to the Miami area. The two groups met, agreed to a peace talk and traded goods. The chief agreed to a peace treaty, but not all was as friendly as it first appeared. It was said that Woolsey tricked the chief and his men into believing he would honor the treaty. Woolsey gave his men a signal to fire their weapons, and many Apache and the chief were killed.

Another version of the tragedy states that about fifty men from an army detachment packed five days' worth of hard tack and bacon before they entered the mountains on foot. Each man carried one blanket over his shoulder, containing the chow of tack and bacon and about sixty rounds of ammunition. The horse and pack team and the guard traveled the base of the mountains. Their destination? The upper wheat fields of Pinal Creek.

The troops continued to climb the Pinal Mountain Range looking for signs of smoke or fires of the nearby Apache camp. The diligent soldiers made no fire to cook their bacon, so they devoured it raw. On the third day of travel, around 3:00 or 4:00 in the afternoon, the soldiers observed two Native women on the mountainside gathering mescal. The women were surrounded and captured and forced to lead the troops through the night to their camp, which was completely surrounded before daylight. The Apache camp was located in a basin on the northeastern slope of the Pinal Mountains.

At sunrise, gunfire started, and the vicious killing began. The army troops could see several of the smoldering fires from their position on the hillside. After a number of bullets were fired, there was a charge on the camp from all directions.

The bridge spanning the Bloody Wash in Miami. *From Goodfreephotos.com.*

The brush and rocks were thick throughout the landscape, making the battlefield even more dangerous. One could hear the roar of large .50-caliber carbines echoing through the bushes and rocks.

No one knew the total number of Natives who fell among the brush and stones. As the dead lay on the desert mountain, many bodies were left uncounted. They estimated around two hundred were slain, including women and young boys. None were spared.

Not many people today know about the battle, and not many can say why the Bloody Tanks above Miami are called that. The legend states that "the blood of the Apache ran red in the mountain stream that bisected the later town of Miami."

Today, some superstitious members of the Apache tribe won't cross the area of the canal that divides Live Oak Street from Sullivan Street in fear of the many ghosts of the Apache who were slaughtered at Bloody Tanks.

Live Oak Street/Sullivan Street
Miami, AZ 85539

4
Mysteries of Miami

Miami Library—*Shhh!*

Miami's first library site was constructed when the wives of mining executives needed a place where the members of the Woman's Club could meet and enjoy the classics and cultured ways of life. The club was very active until the Great Depression. At that time, almost everything shut down. There were no movies, no gathering places, so a small library slowly took shape from book donations. It was a great place for people to escape the realities of the world.

After World War II, the old Miami High School gymnasium began to show its wear and tear. A new state-of-the-art gymnasium was built in 1951. It was called the Miami Memorial Gymnasium in honor of the fallen soldiers who once attended the nearby high school. It presented such a fabulous basketball floor that teams like the Phoenix Suns and Harlem Globe Trotters came to town just to play a few games and shoot some hoops.

The Miami Memorial Library moved into the vacant Miami Memorial Gymnasium in November 1969. The classic library truly has the look of an earlier time period: original oak wood furniture, and the shelves and décor are features that one might recall from the 1970s. The Miami Memorial Library is located in the old high school basketball gym. It still houses the wooden gymnasium floors, and the bookshelves were made from the old wooden bleacher benches. There is a Miami High School "sports hall of

The Miami Public Library. *Author's collection.*

fame" in the back part of the library. The glass wall shelving once displayed awards as the prized trophy case.

Grace Guerra and her paranormal team, Ghost to Ghost Arizona, investigated many places in the Globe, Miami area, and one of those locations was the Miami Library. The team put on a seminar, which included a slideshow and a question-and-answer session with anyone in the group who attended the mini event. The gathering was the suggestion of the head librarian at the time, who was one of Grace's friends. After it was over, the paranormal team was allowed to do an investigation of the library. They were even able to enter places that were being renovated, such as the girl's shower room. They placed a digital recorder in the shower and left it to record any voices of spirits that might enter the room. The entrance to the shower area was taped off so no one else could enter and disturb the recording with noise. Meanwhile, the group went back into the library and took several more photographs, hoping to catch an apparition.

Later, when they picked up their digital recorders, they heard two very clear EVPs that said, "Watch this. What's the hub? Bud boys, what's the hub bud boys?" and giggled. The second EVP sounded like the same voice, and it said, "Ouch that hurt!"

The group investigated the Miami Library only one time, but that visit presented some of the clearest EVPs they had ever gathered.

Shhhh—quiet please. Be silent in the library, and perhaps you will hear even more. Check it out. Surely, the spirits are all on the same page.

Miami Memorial Library
282 South Adonis Avenue
Miami, AZ 85539

YMCA

In 1910, the Miami Copper Company formed an alliance with the YMCA to provide recreational and social activities for its employees. A one-story framed building was constructed near the company's concentrator facility, where employees played games of chess, checkers and billiards and relaxed by reading newspapers and magazines.

In 1915, the state territorial YMCA secretary made a deal with company officials to expand the YMCA's facilities and presence within the community. The Miami Copper Company agreed to construct a new, modern $85,000 YMCA building in the heart of the downtown business area. Plans for the new building were drawn up by Henry Jaastad of Tucson. The contract for the construction was given to Briggs and Daniels of Globe.

The new facility was dedicated on May 10, 1917, and the new three-story YMCA building soon became the grand showcase on the corner of Sullivan Street and Miami Avenue. The new YMCA building had a steam-heated indoor swimming pool that made the "old swimming hole look like a relic of old days." The shallow end was three and a half feet deep, the deep end was over eight feet deep.

The new YMCA featured a gymnasium with a stage and even a two-lane bowling alley. It provided twenty-three dormitory-style rooms with showers for single white men, such as engineers, chemists, accountants and other specialists and employees of the Miami Copper Company. There was a banquet room, complete with a furnished modern kitchen, conference room and a library and reading room. Billiard tables outlined the spacious lobby, which was accented with a fireplace. YMCA members had access to all the facilities. Later, the Boys and Girls Clubs were added for afternoon games after school, scout meetings and swimming lessons. The building

The YMCA building in Miami, Arizona. *Author's collection.*

remained segregated until sometime after World War II. First aid classes to prevent drowning were taught by instructors. The room was ventilated in the summer and warmed in the winter.

Tom Foster of Bullion Plaza Cultural Center escorted Debe Branning, Cindy Lee and Vicki Galli on a VIP tour of the old YMCA facility. Debe was impressed with the size of the building and the fact that it once had its own two-lane bowling alley. She was not impressed, however, with the narrow walkway on one side of the now empty swimming pool. "I had to walk on the other side of the pool, where the walkway is wider. All I kept thinking about were children being pushed off the narrow side and into the water, thrashing around and doing their best to swim to the edge!"

Lynette Hughes, who grew up in Miami, recalled the fearful feelings she had while taking swimming lessons at the YMCA as a child. "I almost drowned in that pool when I was in the fifth grade."

Debe Branning nodded in agreement. Having lived across the street from a city pool in Nebraska, she understood the anxiety of taking swimming lessons from stern Red Cross instructors and the fear of being pushed into the deep end of the pool and not being able to swim to safety. "Perhaps there is trapped energy lingering in the walls of the old YMCA swimming pool, too!"

Wendy Clark with GHOST (Ghost Hunters of Southern Tucson) Crew mentioned something that happened when the team investigated the YMCA.

Left: The YMCA swimming pool. *Author's collection.*

Right: The staircase to the upstairs gymnasium at the YMCA. *Author's collection.*

> *Something blew in my ear, and I heard a man's voice. My sister and I heard a man laughing with our own ears on the second floor. When we asked if anything bad happened in the building, a shadow came at me in one of the rooms on that second floor. I was asking questions and asked if the man that laughed was in the room with me. We have seen shadows in the auditorium area and voices with our own ears, but the man blowing in my ear and making my hair move and whispering was probably the creepiest thing that happened there.*

Project Paranormal Arizona's Justin Celani reported that their experiences in the old YMCA building were positive ones. If anything, they had a playful feel.

> *When going into the building's gym/stage area, we sat up front and did a rem-pod session. The rem-pod started going crazy and just would not stop. We were sure this was a technical issue, but it was odd, as we never experienced anything like that before. While in that area, we would feel like we were being watched from up about on the second-story bleachers. We continued the investigation, using the rem-pod throughout the night. Everything was normal. We put the rem-pod on the stair post, started walking away and again, the constant beeping sounds started going erratic. This has never happened with the device before and hasn't happened since. At one point, a team member felt like something touched their forehead.*

Rita Olson with Arizona Ghost Adventures offers tour/investigations at the YMCA on a regular basis. Her team has encountered shadow figures moving down hallways, and footsteps have been heard on the gymnasium floor and stage. They tend to get a lot of activity, including disembodied voices, near the empty swimming pool.

> *The para-lights set off really easy near the pool. We feel the activity of children and a lot of their horseplay energy. We have had activity in the shower area and recorded some FLIR images of a person standing there at the entrance. Upstairs, we felt the spirits were people from the past who stayed there when they were younger—perhaps eighteen-year-olds or soldiers back from the war.*

During one of the Ghosts of Globe tours, Vincent Amico of Arizona Paranormal was the lead investigator for haunted tours of the historic YMCA building. Again, the team found that the pool area seemed to hold the residual energy from children who perhaps took swimming lessons and played in the pool. "The children love when we bring out the lighted balls to play." Their team has heard voices throughout the building, especially on the second floor, where they believe family members staying in the living quarters suffered abuse.

Why are so many YMCA buildings haunted? Not only was the YMCA a happy meeting place, but it was also a place where down and out men had a place to go; it was a haven for military men returning from war, sometimes suffering from post-traumatic stress disorder. There were suicides, fires, abuse and occasionally accidents that occurred there. On another note, what better place is there to meet up with "spirited" friends for a game of chess?

YMCA (now known as Miami Mercantile and More, Inc.)
155 North Miami Avenue
Miami, AZ 85539

BULLION PLAZA SCHOOL: LESSONS LEARNED

Miami's Bullion Plaza School in the nearby mining town of Miami, Arizona, is historically important, as it was one of the few schools that educated Mexican American children and dealt with school segregation in Arizona during the early half of the 1900s. The stately Bullion Plaza School was a two-story, reinforced concrete building located on the west end of Miami. The Neo-Classical Revival building was designed by the famed El Paso, Texas architecture firm of Trost and Trost and modeled after El Paso High School, a Neo-Classical Revival building designed by Henry Trost and built in 1916. The Bullion Plaza School was erected in 1923 and has Neo-Classical ornamentation, which includes the central clock, columns with elements from the Ionic order, cornices, pediments, a monumental portico with broad, temple-like steps and a corniced parapet.

The popular school was active from 1923 until the end of the school year of 1994. Its doors were shut due to possible structural safety issues that made the building unsafe for students and the public. The Bullion Plaza School was listed in the National Register of Historic Places on November 27, 2000. Bullion Plaza School was established as a segregated school and was originally constructed to educate the neighboring Native and Mexican American children.

The segregation of Mexican American students was a common practice in Arizona public schools between 1900 and early 1950. This was the same period in which Bullion Plaza School served as a segregated school for Miami's children. Sadly, school administrators of the day believed vocational training schools were needed for Mexican American students because of a perceived idea that they may not have the ability to perform well in traditional scholastic subjects.

The Bullion Plaza School. *Author's collection.*

The formal segregation of Mexican American students in Arizona schools persisted until the early 1950s, when a court decision forced local school districts to drop the practice. This moment also put an end to the segregation of Black students in Arizona as well. This occurred at the same time as the movement to end the segregation of Black people altogether, but the two movements were largely separate. Both, though, had their origins in increasing actions from minority parents who showed that their children's schools were not only separate but inferior, despite the claim of educators and school administrators that segregation was based on the theory of "separate but equal."

Fortunately, the Bullion Plaza School has been resurrected as a historic museum that houses collections and artifacts that reflect the early and modern history of the town and nearby regions. Some of the historic relics from Miami and the surrounding area still hold the energy of their previous owners. The building also houses old war/medical memorabilia and historical cultural exhibits. There has been a lot of unexplained paranormal activity throughout the building, contributing to numerous ghost stories surrounding the museum and former school.

Tom Foster, the current executive director of the Bullion Plaza Cultural Center and Museum, opened up about his perspective of possible hauntings within the building.

> *I have the opportunity of spending long hours, in daylight and darkness, in the old Bullion Plaza School, built in 1923. In that, there is a lot of time for the generations of experiences, both in the normal work environment and, in some instances, beyond the veil of this dimension, to manifest. Most of those experiences are auditory—names being called, greetings and questions. At this point, all of those are from a female spirit that paranormal investigators have begun to call Cecilia. She is just there and gone, and she does not generate any negative feelings.*
>
> *The second floor has a different energy—and not as pleasant! I have seen walking full-body apparitions on cameras placed on the second floor. The energy is best left alone and not intruded on. I stay out of that field of energy after dark. Outside of being just plain creepy, I have nothing to report from the basement. Although many other paranormal groups have had significant experiences there—all of them noted shadow people.*

The second floor is said to be haunted by a malevolent male spirit, which has been known to frighten the staff and some of the visitors. One of the commonly reported apparitions on the first floor, or main floor, is that of a beautiful woman in a flowing white dress who has appeared to staff during the daytime hours as well as late at night.

A local said, "I have seen a small child, the woman ghost and a male figure in this building on several occasions. My sister has seen them, too. This all happened sometime between 1996 and 1999, when the school was still closed for restoration and preservation."

Besides being a school that educated children from first to eighth grade, it is a location that has been through polio outbreaks, tuberculosis and an attempted murder in the lobby, and it is reported that some of the children were punished for speaking their Native language.

Paranormal tour group Arizona Ghost Adventures has experienced orbs, objects being moved, voices, flashlight on-command activity, K2 meter hits,

An early view of the Bullion Plaza School. *Courtesy of the Bullion Plaza Cultural Center.*

along with other equipment activity. They also believe there is an active dark spirit energy in the basement that one of their tour guests photographed. Most members of the museum staff refuse to enter the basement alone. They feel the dark, cemented storage area may be hanging on to dark energies left behind by unknown intruders who frequented the catacombs when the building was empty and unattended.

The late Grace Guerra and her paranormal team, Ghost to Ghost Arizona, have done paranormal investigations at several locations in the Globe/Miami area. A longtime resident of Miami, Grace was well respected in the paranormal field for her work. Grace investigated Bullion Plaza a number of times—from the time Tom Foster began renovating it until she fell ill and passed away.

During their first investigation, in 2003, they were testing a digital recorder and a ghost box. They were on the second floor inside the last classroom to the northwest. Grace asked the box questions and received different answers each time. On its own, the spirit box said a police car was going to park outside the building, that it would start raining and that a policeman would wait for them. The spirit box told them he was there now. They were standing by the front doorway, so Arthur walked over to see. Sure enough, a police car was outside, and it began to rain. Arthur walked outside to see who it was, because the officer was parked by his car, and it turned out to be their son-in-law Thomas checking to see if their daughter Sabrina had obtained dinner for the group. Arthur told Grace, and later, when they went over the recording and the answers, it turned out that the first answer was to the last question she asked, and the last answer was to the first question she asked. The answers came from someone who sounded like they had come from a battlefield—mainly a beach landing during World War II—because of the phrases they used to describe the enemy. After talking to Tom, he told Grace that the room below them had held uniforms from the Second World War and other wars.

Through the years, Grace's team saw orbs, shadows, mists and other unexplained things. They saw apparitions of children and recorded EVPs. But one evening proved to be quite active. They went back to the second floor to set up cables to attached video recorders near the top of the stairs. On the way up the stairs, they passed a small mechanical doll that was motion-activated. As they climbed the steps, the doll activated and moved. They naturally thought they had set it off, but Tom assured them the doll was not connected and that there were no batteries in it.

They set up the camcorders with additional IR lights pointing north and south. As they were looking where to point the south camera, they could see down the hallway and saw what looked like a little boy standing in the dark near the other stairway. The boy waved at them and then ducked back into the stairway. They were able to see him because of the reflection of the light from the bottom of the stairway. They walked down the steps to see if anyone was there, but none of the crew on either floor had seen anyone.

Team member Tim connected the cameras to his computer so they could see what the camcorders were recording. Sabrina reported that the camcorder pointing south was off and that the other camcorder looked like it was on the floor. Tim and Arthur went upstairs and found that the south camera's power cord was unplugged and that the north camera was laying on the floor, off its tripod. They put everything back online and started walking down the hallway to the north, because they heard little kids' voices. As they were walking away, Sabrina called them again and announced the south camera was off again. She said it looked like the north camera was rolling slowly, as if it was coming off the tripod. They were only twenty feet away from the camera and went back to find the south camera unplugged again and the north camera hanging off the tripod on the piece of tape that Arthur had used to attach it. They put everything back and asked the spirits to please leave the camcorders alone. They went back down the hallway to check out the room where they thought they had heard the children's voices. They took several photographs and found many anomalies in them.

Grace gathered the group for a smoke break. Tim, Hope, Grace and Tom went outside to smoke while Sabrina, Melissa and Arthur stayed in the lobby. They were discussing what had happened upstairs when Tom came back in, asking what they wanted. Thinking this was odd, they asked him what he was talking about. Tom said someone had called out, "Tom, oh, Tom, can you come here?" They told him that none of them had called to him. Baffled, he said it was not Sabrina's or Melissa's voice, because he would have recognized their tones of voice. He thought they had let someone in the front door and that they were looking for him. The rest of the group came back in the building and said they heard the girls' voices as clear as a bell.

Whomever this young prankster might have been, another team, Arizona Ghost Adventures, experienced something similar. Rita Olsen reported hearing her name in the basement one evening while they were doing a spirit box session.

The Bullion Plaza School. *Courtesy of Carolee Jackson.*

> *We were filming down there when all of a sudden, my flashlight flew off the ledge of the wall. A team member saw a shadow figure in the basement in the room to the right. Another member of the group described it as a black mass trying to manifest and take shape in human form. In the small basement room, their flashlight and speaker were sitting on a ledge for a good amount of time. Once again, the flashlight, along with the speaker, was knocked down to the ground. One of the ghost tour investigation guests was standing near a table where the team's trigger item porcelain doll was securely sitting. A few minutes later, the doll tumbled to the floor and broke into hundreds of pieces.*

Rita also reported seeing a gray mist of a man exploring items in the military room. Do spirits from the old school enjoy pranking the ghost investigators?

Debe Branning attended a group investigation at the school and experienced something on the second floor.

> *I had walked down the hallway where they store some of the Halloween props, such as the wooden coffin. I suddenly felt like I had walked into an energy still holding on to a school scuffle of the past—you know, like when a group of kids gang up on and surround one of the students and start shoving him around. Fists were flying, and you could almost feel the other students chanting, "Fight! Fight! Fight!"*

Rita Olsen remembered one of her tour guests having that identical feeling in that same area of the hallway. This helps validate the strange energy field felt by both women.

After investigating the Bullion Plaza Building, Debe Branning and other paranormal folks in the field feel the building holds in heavy residual energy that plays out acts of violence over and over again. Although there were never any deaths that occurred at the school, the schoolchildren, teachers and staff were firsthand witnesses to horrifying vicious attacks.

When checking old newspapers, Debe found an article about Miami resident Aurora Serna, age eighteen, and Joe Berumen, age twenty-one, who were married sometime in December 1937. The young couple decided to live in the Live Oaks addition with Berumen's parents and family. This marital arrangement seemed to go along respectfully until something went terribly wrong on the afternoon of November 21, 1938.

An argument in the Berumen home evolved, and within minutes, the frightened young bride dashed out of the house, screaming as her father-in-law, Mr. Pastor Berumen, chased her down the road waving a thirty-inch, three-edge Moroccan bayonet.

Aurora acted quickly and ran to the safety of Bullion Plaza School, entering through the right rear door, screaming, "Save me! Save me!" W.L. Longan was the principal of the school and was hard at work in his office when the hysterical Mrs. Berumen ran into the school hallway. Berumen, her father-in-law, was in hot pursuit. Principal Longan rushed out into the hall and attempted to stop Berumen but missed his target when he swung with his fist and lost his balance. Longan dashed into an adjoining room, where he found a club leaning along the wall to use as a weapon.

Pastor Berumen followed Aurora into the classroom of Miss Elma Eckstein, where he fiercely drove the bayonet into Aurora's right shoulder. The blade came out through her left breast. Longan reported that Berumen was attempting to pull the bayonet from his daughter-in-law's shoulder when he entered the room. The man then climbed up through an open window, where he leapt out and fled.

Distraught, Aurora Berumen slowly pulled out the dagger and threw it across the classroom. It slid across the floor and struck a nearby pupil. The point of the bayonet passed through the student's shoe, not damaging the boy's foot.

Aurora Berumen received treatment at Inspiration Hospital for the bayonet wound. She was later sent home, where she soon recovered from the attack. Her father-in-law, Pastor Berumen, was captured in the hills three miles west of Miami and arrested in connection with the stabbing. An assault charge with an attempt to commit murder was filed, and Pastor Berumen later served a short prison sentence.

Can you imagine the looks that were given when Miami mothers asked their children, "How was school today?"

To add to the many unexplained energies found around Bullion School, in September 1925, Jose Gonzales stabbed his wife five times with a pocket knife and then turned the weapon upon himself, inflicting a severe neck wound while several schoolchildren of the Bullion Plaza School looked on. The woman was rushed to the Miami Inspiration dispensary, suffering only flesh wounds, and recovered. Meanwhile, her husband had only a fighting chance to survive.

Could all of the ghostly residual energy be the result of the aftermath of a free-for-all fight on the Bullion Plaza grounds late one evening? It is noted

A vintage image of a snowy Bullion Plaza School. *Courtesy of the Bullion Plaza Cultural Center.*

that a female rioter received a deep gash on her arm while her companion suffered a scalp wound, all supposedly from flying rocks.

It is also said that in the 1970s, a gentleman was found dead inside the old school building on the staircase that leads down from the second floor. Is this the gentleman whom many have heard moaning on recording devices? Perhaps he is seeking answers for his untimely demise.

The Bullion Plaza School building seems to be one of the most active structures in the Gila County area, with lessons just beckoning to be learned by all.

Bullion Plaza Cultural Center
150 North Plaza Circle
Miami, AZ 85539

5

Restaurants and Cafés

El Ranchito Café, Also Known as the Eagle Saloon

A man known only as F.R. Austin shot himself in the head in the Eagle Saloon on May 24, 1902, around 8:30 p.m. Austin, who was about thirty years old, had only come to reside in Globe for about one week, having recently arrived from the mining town of Clifton, Arizona.

Earlier in the day, Austin had tried to procure rough on rats (poison) at Dr. Neissl's drugstore, but it was refused to him by the owner.

Upon entering the Eagle Saloon, he asked George Shanley, who was behind the bar, if he had a pistol to dispose of. Shanley said yes and produced a weapon that had been left there to sell. Austin took the weapon and, finding the chambers empty, asked Shanley what kind of cartridges it shot. Shanley placed five cartridges in front of him on the bar.

The troubled young man took one of the cartridges, and while loading it in the chambers of the six-shooter, he looked very nervous. Shanley suspected that something was terribly wrong and told him, "Give me the gun, and I will show you."

Austin refused and stepped back from the bar. Fearing Austin intended to cause harm, Shanley started heading toward the back of the room. Three other men who were in the saloon at the time bolted for the screen door at the back, which was stuck fast. Before they could exit the building, Austin placed the six-shooter against his head and fired. He must have used his left

El Ranchito Café. *Courtesy of LeeAnn Powers.*

hand, as the bullet entered the left side of his head and came out on the right side in front of the ear. Death was instantaneous.

Acting coroner Rawlings viewed the body and had it removed to the morgue. The facts as stated were revealed at the inquest. Not a lot of information was uncovered about this man of mystery. Austin was a painter. In his pockets were paint, brushes and a small whiskey flask filled with turpentine. On the flask was the name of a Clifton liquor dealer. There was no money on his person. The body was buried in the pauper cemetery the next afternoon by William Zimmerman at the expense of the county.

Those who have worked in the El Rancho Café in recent years report hearing the back screen door opening and slamming shut. One staff member noted that the same door often closes and acts as though it is stuck, possibly locked by some unseen force. A ghostly cowboy has been seen standing in the rear of the building near the exit. Could the ghost of Austin still be looking for a way out of his troubled life?

El Ranchito Café
686 North Broad Street
Globe, AZ 85501

LA CASITA CAFÉ

The masons in the Globe area were the first to use the upper story of the building above the popular St. Elmo Hotel and Bar in 1879. It is often said that the legendary Big Nose Kate of Tombstone fame later leased the north side of the building and ran a brothel upstairs in the 1880s. The working ladies had "hidey holes" cut in the floorboards to stash their money and goods. Some of the secret hiding spots remain in the upstairs rooms today.

The building was later known as Club Verde and was situated on the edge of Chinatown in the vicinity of Globe's infamous hanging tree. Club Verde had a reputation of one of the rough-and-tumble saloons in Gila County, and at least one murder occurred inside the establishment.

Former owners Pedro and Salustia Reynoso opened the legendary La Casita Café there in 1947. It was a branch of the Guayo's El Ray that came onto the scene in 1938, and its delicious recipes are still prepared today by the third generation of La Casita restaurateurs in Globe and Miami. Recently, Liz Villalobos and fourth-generation restaurateur Annie Villalobos stepped in to continue the legacy of making amazing Mexican food in Globe.

La Casita Café on Broad Street is rumored to be haunted. Guests and waitstaff have all witnessed a mysterious male presence, perhaps an old miner or cowboy, in the lady's restroom. The ghostly man has been seen standing inside the bathroom near the door, which frightens unsuspecting female patrons.

Although the owners of La Casita can safely declare that the spirits in the café are harmless, it should be mentioned that previous paranormal investigators and sensitives feel there is a female spirit by the name of Lady Rose that frequently pays a visit to the building.

La Casita Café. *Courtesy of Carolee Jackson.*

Left: La Casita is known for its haunted bathroom. *Author's collection.*

Right: La Casita's upstairs door to the brothel. *Author's collection.*

One afternoon, MVD Ghostchasers Debe Branning and Shiela McCurdy stopped to have lunch at La Casita Café. It wasn't very busy, so they knew it was probably a good time to ask about the restaurant's ghosts and unexplained hauntings. Before long, the owner-manager was escorting the ladies up to the second floor, the former living quarters of the Reynosa family. "You can still see the old brothel rooms that were upstairs before my family moved in," she explained.

How could they say no? Debe and Shiela were whisked through the kitchen, out the back door and instructed to climb a very weathered wooden ladder to the rooftop over the kitchen. Then they jumped down three feet into a doorway and a hallway that led to the old second-floor living quarters.

There were still remnants of the old, peeling wallpaper, faux carpeting painted onto the linoleum floors and an old claw bathtub in a washroom. The women ventured down a hallway that led to a doorway that divided the two businesses in the building. All the upper-floor rooms on both sides were used as a hotel and brothel. Employees at the café have felt the unpleasant feeling of someone watching them in the dark hallways.

A gentleman by the name of Sam Bucker once worked as a bartender at St. Elmo's. On July 4, 1910, Bucker was found dead in his room on the second floor. He died of heart failure due to acute alcoholism. Is Sam Bucker's spirit the mysterious male presence that patrons have encountered near the restroom?

The second floor has been used for restaurant storage in recent times, but at one time, it was the early home of the Reynoso family. Nana Reynoso sat down with Debe and recalled a time when her family may have encountered their own ghostly paranormal experience. It was very late. The café was closed for the night and the staff had finished cleaning duties and left for home. The family had locked the doors and gone upstairs to call it a night. All was calm and quiet. Suddenly, they began to hear noises coming from downstairs. Furniture was being moved around, and glasses and bottles clinked while voices reveled as though there was a party. The family immediately headed downstairs to confront the intruders—only, the dining room was completely dark and vacant. It seemed the ghosts of St. Elmo's had something to celebrate just one more time.

La Casita Café
470 North Broad Street
Globe, AZ 85501

6

PLACES OF BUSINESS

THE MINE HARDWARE AND SUPPLY COMPANY BUILDING

Two Globe businessmen, Bracco and Giacoma, constructed a new building on the southwest corner of Broad and Oak Streets in 1915. Designed in a Vernacular architecture style, the commercial building was in a prime location. It was originally designed to house the Mine Hardware and Supply Company, which moved into the building in 1918.

The Mine Hardware and Supply Store boasted pressed tin ceilings, hardwood floors and even an elevator. The walls had shelves that reached from the floor to the fourteen-foot-tall ceiling, with rolling ladders on rails attached to the ceiling. The ladders made it convenient for shopkeepers to reach hardware supplies stored on high shelving bins.

W.A. Sullivan was the president and treasurer of the company for several years. Ed L. Bitner came on as an employee in 1935, worked his way up the ladder and later served on the board of directors. After Sullivan's death, Bitner became the president of the company, and it was family-owned for many years.

The building has also been the home of Hansen's Clothing Store, the Richelieu Café and the White House Hotel. The comfortable White House Hotel offered accommodations to early businessmen and mining officials who traveled to Globe. James L. Bracco died upstairs in the White House Hotel on New Year's Day, January 1, 1942, at the age of sixty-seven. He had suffered a stroke triggered by a cerebral hemorrhage.

In 1984, the store was rented out, with a flower shop located in the rear of the building. Soon, the owners began to report ghostly activity. The employees were often frightened in the late evening hours by the sound of heavy steps coming from the front of the store and traveling to the back area, where they were working. They checked for intruders in the building but found no customers or other workers.

The building's basement was later used by the owners to publish a small newspaper. Ironically, the newspaper employees also heard the mysterious heavy footsteps. Again, they were startled by the sound of someone walking overhead from the front of the building to the back, stopping abruptly. Since there was not supposed to be anyone upstairs, the newspaper staff wasted hours running upstairs late at night to confirm there were never any intruders, just the heavy footsteps of an unseen ghost.

Still later, the store was moved to another location, and the main floor was renovated for county and state offices. During later renovations, workmen would come to the building each morning, only to find their ladders and tools had been moved around to a different area of the structure during the night. Could this have been the ghost of James Bracco still minding the store in this historic Globe building? Or is he reliving his final years, when he was a

Mine and Hardware Supply's building echoes with sounds of moving ladders and bowling balls. *Author's collection.*

The scene of a tragic accident with a horse at the Mine and Hardware Supply building. *Courtesy of the "Growing up Globe" Facebook page.*

resident of the White House Hotel? Bracco was a very civic-minded resident of Globe in his early years, having been elected as a city councilman. His life was threatened many times, as he was not afraid to stand up and say what he felt. Maybe his ghost has unfinished business in Globe and the old Mine Supply and Hardware building.

Or could the ghost be that of the unfortunate man who met his fate outside of the front door of the building. Judge John McBride, whose titles included federal mediator in the Globe/Miami copper strike troubles and the only ex-president of the American Federation of Labor, was killed on October 18, 1917, when a runaway horse kicked him through the plate-glass window of the Mine Supply and Hardware building.

Judge McBride was casually standing on the corner of Broad and Oak Streets at the time. Suddenly a saddle horse, owned by the W.W. Brookner Company and ridden by employee A.G. Hayes, charged down Broad Street, throwing the rider to the pavement. The crazed, riderless horse dashed down the street for roughly 150 feet. Its head was lowered as it viciously bucked, apparently blinded with rage. As the horse attempted to round the corner, its hoof struck the cement sidewalk. It stumbled, and its feet went out from under him. The runaway horse fell and rolled near Judge McBride. In the animal's scramble to get back up to its feet, it kicked McBride in the pit of his stomach, hurling him through a heavy plate-glass show window.

The judge lay with head and shoulders impaled in the show window. As the horse struggled to regain its feet, it ground the man's body against the saw-edged shards of glass remaining in the window frame. Jagged bits of broken glass tore the flesh around his lower extremities to shreds and severed arteries, from which great quantities of blood spouted. First aid treatment was immediately administered by the clerk of the board of supervisors Frank L. Gates and J. Wilson Stone, an employee of Hansen's Clothing Store in the Old Mine Supply and Hardware Building.

The injured man died of shock and blood loss from severed arteries at the county hospital. His shattered body was taken back to Wayne County, Ohio, for burial. Judge John McBride was widely known and beloved not only in this district but also throughout the entire country, and he had, for many years, identified nationally with the union labor movement.

Stand on the corner of Broad and Oak Streets, and perhaps you will discover residual energy from Globe's violent past. Listen for broken glass and the sound of the hooves in the light of day.

"Most horses don't walk backwards voluntarily—because what they can't see doesn't exist."
—*Soul Music*, Terry Pratchett

The Old Mine Supply and Hardware Building
100 South Broad Street
Globe, AZ 85501

THE OLD DOMINION COMMERCIAL COMPANY BUILDING

One of the most haunted buildings in Globe is the Old Dominion Commercial Company building, located at 190 North Broad Street. In the late 1870s, people began to move to the new mining camp called Globe. One of these settlers was a man named Alonzo Bailey. Bailey and G.S. Van Wagenen opened a general store on Broad Street. Eventually, Bailey established his own general merchandise store and called it the Old Dominion Commercial Company, located on the corner of Broad and Mesquite Streets.

The Old Dominion Commercial Company became one of the top businesses on Broad Street. It sold groceries, dry goods, clothing and more. Bailey even opened a bank in the store that was very successful.

Future Arizona governor George W.P. Hunt worked at the Old Dominion Commercial Company as a delivery boy in the 1890s and eventually became a clerk, then later manager of the grocery department. Hunt was eventually promoted to secretary and then president of the corporation.

The current structure was built in 1904 and was designed in a Neoclassical Vernacular architectural style. In 1928, the JCPenney Company moved into the building and became a prominent fixture on Broad Street into the mid-1990s. Women who worked in the store diligently straightened the shelves, tables and racks before going home at the end of their shift. The next morning, they would find the store in complete disarray.

There are rumors of several ghosts existing in the old building, mainly on the second floor. They say a man who was the store's bookkeeper is still searching for a missing set of ledger books. He has been heard walking around the top floor. During a renovation of the building in the late 1990s, an old set of ledger books was found tucked between the walls of one of the rooms. Was this the set of misplaced ledgers the frazzled bookkeeper was searching for?

The Old Dominion Commercial building today. *Author's collection.*

Some have also heard disembodied sobs and the cries of a young girl on the upper floor. During renovations, the owners lived upstairs while they worked on the main floor below. Their daughter was often visited by a spirit who liked to move her possessions around the room. Was it the ghost of a young girl reliving her lost youth?

Dominion Commercial Company
101 North Broad Street
Globe, AZ 85501

THE OLD DOMINION MINE PARK: THE TALE OF THE PECULIAR LOCKET

The skeleton remains—the bones of the Old Dominion Mine—can still be spotted flush along the hills that were the backdrop of the former epic mining company. Resembling the forgotten mine in the recent *Ghostbusters: Afterlife* movie (2021), the historic grounds are something to see. Most of the historic buildings are long gone, but something just as valuable is now in their place, a gathering spot for local citizens, visiting tourists and children.

The Old Dominion Mine was active from 1882 to 1931, when Miami/Globe grew from just a few prospectors looking to gain riches into a thriving mining community. Once the Old Dominion Mine shut down in 1931, folks passed around the idea of turning the area into a community park. This finally became a reality in 2000.

It is a great resource for teaching the history of the site and local mining development. Walk along one of the many trails or grab a seat on a bench and feel the energy of former mine workers, such as the Serbian Verisovitz brothers.

Elise and Mojorani Verisovitz reunited in Globe after a separation in Serbia eighteen years prior (1898). For many years afterward, they had sought each other out in the United States and unexpectedly met face to face in the underground workings of a copper mine near Globe, Arizona.

Elise had left the family home in Kafodar along the banks of the Terherna River of Serbia in 1898 to seek his fortune in the mystical and far away land of America. After many adventures and hardships, the wanderer obtained work in Butte, Montana, as a mucker. There, the exiled man worked for a number of years, sending regular remittances to his parents in Kafodar.

Ruins of the Old Dominion Mine. *Courtesy of Carolee Jackson.*

A Dominion Mine postcard. *From Wikimedia.*

The Dominion Mine produced copper from 1880 to 1931. *Courtesy of the Bullion Plaza Cultural Center.*

When his younger brother Mojorani reached adulthood, he decided to head to America to find his brother from whom he'd received money, the sum of which was not to be earned in Kafodar. Upon his departure, the venturesome youngster was given a locket of a peculiar design by his mother, a replica of which had been presented to Elise when he had left so many years before.

While searching for his older sibling, Mojorani made his way to Butte, but his brother was not to be found, as he had left Montana some time before. The younger brother then secured a position and contributed to the family exchequer. For a number of years, Mojorani sought word of Elise, who had apparently vanished.

The younger brother eventually gave up the search for Elise and came to work at the mines in Globe.

While working underground, Mojorani noticed a man observing the peculiarly shaped locket he wore around his neck. At length, the observer spoke. It was Elise. He had recently returned to the United States after working as a miner in Peru.

After traveling thousands of miles, two brothers were reunited by an accidental discovery in the 1,400-foot level of the Old Dominion Mine in 1916. The two men had been separated for eighteen years, and their meeting underground is a twist of fate that bears out the old adage that "truth is stranger than fiction"

Old Dominion Historic Mine Park
161 North Murphy Street
Globe, AZ 85501

WAILING GHOSTS OF COPPER HILL ROAD

In March 1908, evidence of a horrible crime was discovered by miners employed by the Globe Consolidated Company near Copper Hill, situated about one mile west of Globe, Arizona. The men found the skeletal remains of a woman buried in a crevice in the rocks on the mining claim near Copper Hill Road.

The gruesome discovery was reported to Judge Thomas and the sheriff's office, and an investigation was immediately started.

The miners who made the discovery were conducting assessment work on the Baltimore Claim for the Globe Consolidated Company. There was a crevice in the rocks about thirty feet from the Copper Hill Road that showed indications of mineralization, and the men had been instructed to excavate in the fissure. When about six feet of dirt had been removed, the miners discovered an old, rusty bedspring. Directly underneath the bedspring was a row of weathered boards. Somewhat mystified, the men removed the springs and boards and found the skeleton. The men immediately stopped their excavation and notified authorities.

There was a hole in the skull that had been made by a blunt weapon. A pick was found lying near the body and was thought to be the instrument of murder. A pair of women's shoes were lying near the bones and were accepted as evidence that it was the skeleton of a woman. Other nearby signs indicated that the crime had been committed several years prior and that perhaps the woman had been lured to the vicinity by the slayer, who murdered her with a blow from the pick.

Copper Hill's post office was established in June 1908 and discontinued in February 1933. Copper Hill once had five hundred residents serving the nearby mines. Copper Hill had a hospital, school, mercantiles and shops, boardinghouses, offices and places of business. The Great Depression marked the end of the town, and all that remains are foundations.

The Copper Hill Mill site is home to several ruins (some on private property) that can be reached with rigorous hiking. The mill is large, with an underground passage and tunnels. Do not enter without permission and proper exploration gear.

Ghosts have been reported in the area of Copper Hills. Some of the residents nearby claim they have heard strange sounds, such as crying or screaming. Could this be the eerie haunt of the lady who was found buried beneath the bedsprings?

Copper Hill Road
Globe, AZ 85501

BIZARRE ACCIDENT AT MCGOWEN MACHINE WORKS

John B. Tordiff was working at night in a Globe auto establishment when he fell victim to a bizarre accident. The man died from strangulation after a part of his work shirt became caught in the machinery he was working with. Held by the collar band, the upper part of his cotton shirt became caught on the cogs of a drill press and drawn tighter and tighter around his neck until the man could no longer breathe and lost consciousness.

Tordiff was found dead in the workshop the following morning, the machinery still in the on position. It had only ceased operating when the gas engine was depleted. Since he was unable to free himself from the equipment, it was declared Tordiff had died of strangulation.

The body of Tordiff was discovered as described shortly after 9:30 a.m. by A.E. Lewis, who had gone to the shop to have some repair work done. Lewis testified at the inquest hearing that he did not examine the body but observed that Tordiff's shirt had been caught on a nail that was fastened to the machine and was drawn tight around his neck, apparently choking him to death.

Lewis stated that Tordiff must have been dead for several hours. He immediately notified others, and the body was released from the drill press and removed to the undertaking rooms of F.L. Jones and Son. The body was rigid, indicating that Tordiff had indeed been dead for many hours. It was presumed that he must have been working late Friday night and that the accident, resulting in his death, occurred around 9:00 p.m. or later. The gasoline engine that powered the drill press continued to run until the gas was finally exhausted and was heard as late as 3:00 in the morning. The belt was detached from the drill press; whether it was detached by Tordiff in his effort to save himself could not be determined. From the appearance of things, Mr. Tordiff tried to disconnect the clutch connecting the drill press to the power and then, in some manner, became caught in the machine.

The inquest was held at 3:00 the following afternoon before Justice W.C. McKenzie, the acting coroner. The witnesses examined were Charles Collins; A.E. Lewis; Dr. B.G. Fox, county physician; Otto Kean; Charles Lloyd; and W.W. Cunningham, chief of police.

Charles Collins, who was well acquainted with the deceased, testified that he had known him since 1911 and thought he was about sixty years old. He said he did not know if the deceased had any relatives besides an uncle living on a ranch near Butte, Montana, which Tordiff claimed to own.

The McGowen Machine Shop. *Author's collection.*

Dr. Fox testified that he had examined the body and that Tordiff had died of strangulation. There were marks of the cogwheel and grease on the shirt and vest he was wearing. He judged that Tordiff had been dead for at least eight to ten hours—possibly twelve hours. The body was rigid.

Otto Kean testified that he had known Tordiff for three or four years, observed the body on the drill press and was certain Tordiff had been drawn into the machinery. Tordiff occupied himself by doing lathe work and certain auto repairs in a little shop known as the Novelty Machine Works (now known as the McGowen Machine Works) located near the Arizona Easter Depot. Kean said he was in the shop on Friday and noticed there were several nails stuck in the machine. He felt like speaking to Tordiff about the nails but feared he would resent hearing about the pending danger.

The testimony of other witnesses was corroborative and brought out no new facts.

Justice McKenzie and Constable Childress examined the belongings of the deceased at his shop and the small house in which he roomed in Kinney Park. Two small wallets were found in a satchel and contained $23.03, and in a trunk, there was a withdrawal card from Damon Lodge, Knights of Pythias of Butte Montana, dated December 2, 1907, and another from the Western Federation of Labor, Engineers Union No. 83 of Butte dated August 31, 1909. There were no letters or other papers discovered to indicate that Tordiff had any relatives.

After the inquest, Charles Collins informed Justice McKenzie that he had talked with Tordiff only a few days before his death and that in the discussion, he had mentioned the possibility of a railroad strike. Tordiff had remarked that he had no reason to worry, that he did not owe anyone a cent and had $900 saved. Tordiff had no account with any of the local banks, and Collins felt sure that he had hidden his money in a secret location and that a more thorough search should be made of his room and shop. Acting on this information, Childress and Collins made a further investigation and found in Tordoff's room $900 in a bill book hidden on a shelf under some papers. The money was turned over to Sheriff Kinsey and placed in his safe.

The coroner's jury, composed of C.A. Wind, foreman; G.B. Ruiz; J.R. Stanifell; R.L. Lapington; W.H. Mercer; C.M. Williams; and D.L. Edwards, rendered a verdict in accordance with the facts and stated that he came to his death after being caught by a nail that held a boring attachment to the spindle of the drill press, said nail becoming caught in his shirt, winding around until death was caused by strangulation, which was the result of his own personal negligence.

Tordiff, originally from Scranton, Pennsylvania, was known to be a highly skilled machinist and had held many responsible positions in Butte and elsewhere. Among them was the position of master mechanic for large mining companies. He had lived in Globe for about eleven years. He had a reserved disposition and made very few friends.

Efforts were made to locate his uncle, who was supposed to reside at Butte, Montana, and to ascertain whether he had any other relatives before arrangements were made for the funeral. John Tordiff was buried in the Globe Cemetery.

McGowen Machine Works
202 West Oak Street
Globe, AZ 85501

ARIZONA BAKERY: THE NEED FOR DOUGH

Louis Berndt and Koch, the proprietors of the Globe Bakery, moved into a newly completed building at the corner of Broad and Cedar Streets in June 1909. The gentlemen were proud of being the pioneer bakers of Globe, and their new bakery was modernly equipped. The new ovens had a capacity of twelve thousand loaves of bread and five hundred pies every twenty-four hours.

Upstairs was the Globe Bakery Hall, which offered dances, celebrations and lectures with the likes of Professor M.F. Knox, the founder of the Mental Science College of Seattle. Koch purchased a fine piano and installed it in the hall above the bakery.

Later, the upstairs space would be converted into the Hotel Ardon. Several small families of Globe and schoolteachers would rent the rooms set off a long hallway.

Joseph Blessent and Company, the proprietors of the Arizona Bakery, purchased the Globe Bakery Building in September 1919 from Berndt and operated a new bakery and delicatessen under the firm name of the Arizona Bakery.

Joe Blessent met with an instant, horrible death at 7:20 a.m. on December 3, 1920. While doing his usual task of overseeing the big motor-driven dough mixing machine in the bakery, it was necessary for him to recover a paddle he dropped while scraping some surplus dough from the sides of the machine into the moving mass of dough. Standing on a box and reaching for the paddle was his last act. It was presumed that he leaned an inch too far in to pick the paddle out of the mixer; his left arm was then drawn into the seething vortex of dough, dragging his entire body into the machine. The accident happened so fast that the unfortunate man barely had time to cry out, the metal paddles of the machine striking the left side of his head, tearing their way down his left side to his hip, horribly mangling his body.

Martin Sanderetta, an employee of the bakery, was standing nearby at the time of the accident and immediately pulled the switch that controlled the power. He attempted to lift Blessent from the machine but discovered this to be impossible, as his entire body, except for his head, was buried in the dough. His head was badly mangled, and almost every bone in his body was broken. Sanderetta ran out to the street and called for help. Several people responded, and after much difficulty, the body was removed and taken immediately to the Jones and Son undertaking parlors.

The Arizona Bakery's building has its secrets. *Author's collection.*

Blessent was born in Italy and was about forty-two years old at the time of his death. He was well known and well liked in the community. He helped to finance many business enterprises in the district and owned a considerable amount of property on Euclid Avenue in Globe. He had several family members in Globe, including a favorite niece of his who did office work for the baker.

He was buried in the Globe Cemetery. His death has remained a mystery—and then there was his will, but more on that later.

The Arizona Bakery and Hotel Ardon building sits on the northeast corner of Cedar and Broad Streets.

Arizona Bakery (currently various businesses)
275 North Broad Street
Globe, AZ 85501

GLOBE POST OFFICE: MYSTERIOUS TUNNELS AND BULLET HOLES

The United States Post Office and federal courthouse in downtown Globe was built in 1926. The building served historically as a courthouse of the United States District Court of the District of Arizona. Several high-profile cases were tried in the building. The post office reflects Beaux Arts architecture. It was listed in the National Register of Historic Places in 1985.

A vintage image of the Globe Post Office. *From Pinterest.*

It's a good example of the Federal design in the Neo-Classical style. It was built using red brick with stone and concrete enhancements. The design included a balustrade at the roof, a simple cornice, keystones, quoins and other decorative features. Two Doric columns border the main entrance, and a symbolic stone eagle gazes down from a pediment above the entrance. It is located just one block north of the train depot—a requirement by the government to aid in mail transportation by rail.

Retired mail carrier Justin Brandt was employed by the U. S. Post Office for over thirty-five years and has an endless amount of knowledge of its true history and can ramble off stories of its past. Brandt informed the tour guests that there is a sister building to the Globe Post Office located in Port Angeles, Washington.

Each April, Brandt led his public tour of the building and escorted guests to the normally closed, off-limits areas of the historic post office. These areas included the former civil defense room downstairs and the building's third floor, which featured the federal courthouse. The entire basement was once considered a probable fallout shelter during the panic of the Cold War in the 1960s. During this troubled time, it was feared the United States would be a target of a nuclear bomb. Immediately, businesses and homeowners created fallout shelters in their basements and backyards. It was necessary to make citizens prepared for an emergency. It was said that several hundred people could be sheltered in the post office building. There is still one highly secured room in the basement where the civil defense rations were stored. Here, you can still find a display of water ration cans, lanterns, gas masks and inedible cracker wafers to sustain oneself during a crisis.

The basement offices of the post office were the locations where locals would come to get their social security cards, passports and marriage licenses, apply for citizenship or meet with the immigration offices. Young men signed up for the draft and visited the enlistment office here.

Brandt noted that the upstairs light fixtures were original, although rewired for today's standards. Wood paneling and carpeting were features added upstairs around 1977. Guests can gaze at the stained glass inset in the soaring ceilings of the former grand courtroom on the second floor. They were originally part of skylights that allowed light to shine in through the glass.

Brandt's once-a-year public post office tour was always a must-do during the annual Globe home tour. The highlight of the tour was the opportunity to enter through the secret door and observe the mysterious hidden black tunnel that circled over the operating post office. Everything

The Globe Post Office holds many secrets. *Courtesy of Carolee Jackson.*

was painted black—yes, black—including the doors, the ceiling, the walls and the floors.

The only person who was allowed to enter the door to the black tunnels was the postal inspector or the U.S. marshal. There was a ladder that an employee could use to climb to an additional black catwalk when needed. Every few feet, there was a vent-like window that spied on the post office workers in their locker rooms and workspaces below, somewhat like a security camera system would operate today. Of course, after the employee privacy acts came into existence in the 1960s, it became illegal to spy on employees—especially in dressing rooms—so the secret windows were painted black, never to see the light at the end of the tunnel again.

Brandt liked to spook the schoolchildren who came on the tour by leading one of the students to the secret door and offering them the chance to open it and turn on the lights. Of course, there would always be a creepy Halloween cut-out ghost dangling from the ceiling, followed by shrieks and giggles from the children.

But what is probably the most mysterious story in the building concerns bullet holes in the banister on the stairway that leads to the federal courtroom. No one really knows why they are there or how they ended up in the building. Many speculate from a story that may or not have happened that a suspect squirmed out of their handcuffs, hit the federal marshal and made a run for freedom. Shots were fired, and the story goes on to say that the suspect was hit three times out of the seven shots fired by the marshal and then fell over the railing to their death. Two of the bullet holes are actually still in the railing, along with one of the slugs. None of the local historians could confirm this event, although most of them have heard the tale as well. Maybe someday, someone who was in the courtroom that day will come forward and end this mystery—right now, there are too many holes in the story to be true.

Globe Post Office
101 South Hill Street
Globe, AZ 85501

7
CEMETERIES

Globe Cemetery

The Globe Cemetery sits on a hill just north of the Globe historic downtown district. Established in 1876 and still in use today, it is laid out in sections, with a section for the Elks, the Knights of Pythias and the Buffalo Soldiers. There are also sections for the Chinese, Italian and Slavic families who helped settle the area. Many of the earliest burials were those of newcomers attracted by opportunities in mining. They now lie with bandits, gunslingers, prominent businessmen, ranchers, housewives and working girls.

Some of the famous memorials include those of:

- Phin Clanton: The second-born son of "Old Man" Clanton who was part of the Earp saga.
- Al Sieber: A veteran of the Civil War and, for twenty years, a leader of scouts for the U.S. Army in Arizona.
- Glenn Reynolds: A man killed in the line of duty against the Apache in 1889.
- John H. Thompson: A Gila County sheriff for eight terms, from 1890 to 1912. He survived various shootouts.
- Robert S Knowles: A scout to Al Sieber and a friend of the Apache Kid.

- Judge Anton Hackney: The founder and editor of the *Arizona Silver Belt* newspaper.
- Thomas B. Hammond: A prospector killed by the Apache in 1876 and the first to be buried in Globe Cemetery.

The U.S. veterans buried in the cemetery were veterans of the Apache Wars, the Civil War, the Spanish-American War, World War I, World War II, the Korean War and the Vietnam War. Buffalo Soldiers are also buried here. Hundreds of early pioneers from the area are also buried in the Globe Cemetery.

Hermann Wolf, the old gravedigger of the Globe Cemetery, found himself in big trouble in August 1904 after he exhumed the corpse of Brigia Alvarez, who died on August 1, 1904. The idea that the woman was really alive when she was buried got possession of Wolf and one or two of his friends, even though several hours had elapsed since the interment. Wolf and a companion returned to the cemetery and dug up the body. When the coffin was opened, nothing unnatural was discovered in the appearance of the body to suggest a premature burial. However, Arizona has a statute making it a felony to disinter a human body without the proper legal authority. A charge was filed against Wolf, and he was arrested and given a hearing. After it was shown that his intentions were humane, Wolf was admonished by the court and discharged.

Debe Branning recalled visiting the Globe Cemetery while creating yet another route for the Cemetery Crawl she organizes each year—her version of the *Amazing Race*. She and Kenton Moore were scouting for the grave marker of Phin Clanton when she noticed a middle-aged man digging at one of the gravestones in the same area. She watched him for a while and eventually approached him to ask for directions to Clanton's grave.

"Oh, I bet you are wondering what I am doing out here all alone digging up a grave," he wiped his brow.

"It did cross my mind," Debe nodded.

He told her that he had come out to tidy the area of his grandmother's burial plot. The ground was sinking, and the large granite stone posts had been tipped over. He had decided to dig down to rebury the granite posts and secure them in the ground once again. Debe was relieved. He wasn't a grave robber after all.

"Could you please direct me to the grave marker of Phin Clanton?" she asked. "I would love to get a photograph of it."

The gentleman put down his shovel and pointed.

Right: The grave marker of Phin Clanton (1843–1906). *Author's collection.*

Below: The grave marker of E.L Ferguson (Pete Spence, 1851–1914). *Author's collection.*

"You are only a few feet away!" He walked over to the gravestone and gave her a history lesson.

Pete Spence, also known as Elliot Larkin Ferguson, was a known stagecoach robber and one of the suspected murderers of Morgan Earp. The gunfighter occasionally served the Old West as a lawman. He became good friends with the Clanton family and rode with the notorious "cowboys." Spence once lived in Tombstone, and his house sat directly across the street from the Earps. Spence partnered with Frank Stillwell on various business ventures—both good and bad.

After that famous gunfight at the OK Corral on October 26, 1881, the Clanton Gang took their revenge by orchestrating the murder of Morgan Earp. Both Stillwell and Pete Spence were named as suspects in his death. The indictment of Spence was eventually dropped. Soon, Earp began his vendetta ride of revenge. Spence turned himself in just to seek protection from the Earps' wrath. He later committed manslaughter and spent prison time at the Yuma Territorial Prison in 1893. Later, Pete Spence operated a goat ranch with his old friend Phin Clanton. He lived out his later years in Globe, Arizona.

Phineas Clanton was also a member of the "cowboys," but he was able to stay out of the spotlight for most of his roughhousing days. He was accused of being a part of the ambush shooting of Virgil Earp. Phineas was later released, since there was no concrete evidence of his presence. He did serve a prison term at the Yuma Territorial Prison for cattle rustling.

Clanton returned to ranching and married a widow named Mrs. Bohme and helped raise her twelve-year-old son, William. Phineas became a respectable goat rancher near Globe and stayed on the right side of the law. Phin was caught in a heavy snowstorm in the hills near his home in 1905. He became ill and died in January 1905 from exposure. He was buried in the Globe Cemetery. At the time, his grave was enclosed by a heavy picket fence.

A few years later, Pete Spence returned to Globe and eventually married the widowed Clanton in 1910. Spence died in Globe in 1914 and was buried in the plot next to Phin Clanton. The two men, who were outlaws together in life, are now buried side by side—together again in death. It is said that at one time, Spence's grave was marked by a wooden cross. Weather and time decayed the primitive tombstone, and there is no longer any indicator on the barren plot.

Why was there never a new tombstone erected at his grave? Why is there a memorial gravesite and marker placed across the roadway? Which grave actually contains the remains of Pete Spence?

"Some folks say they decided it was best to leave Pete Spence's grave unmarked back then," the gentleman told Debe. "They were afraid someone would come along and desecrate his grave for murdering Morgan Earp. But the widow buried her husbands, the two best friends, side by side—and they set up a decoy, marked with his real name, E.L. Ferguson, across the road."

As a dowser, Debe wanted to solve this mystery once and for all. Was the gravesite next to Clanton occupied by Spence? Was there someone buried in the plot across the narrow road from Clanton's grave? She packed a set of dowsing rods in her bag and planned to conduct a little experiment at the grave sites of Phineas Clanton and Pete Spence.

> *I took out the dowsing rods and waited for the breeze to fade. I stood at the foot of the plot indicating E.L. Ferguson "Spence" was buried "somewhere in the vicinity" and held the dowsing rods in both hands facing forward. I asked the rods to cross as I walked over a body. I walked forward slowly over the top of the plot. The rods remained straight forward. I stood on top of the grass and raised the rod in my right hand high above my head. I asked the rods to indicate if a male or female rested in the grave. The rod remained neutral.*

Then she began part two of the experiment. Debe stepped back across the road to the foot of the unmarked grave, where Spence is allegedly buried. Holding both rods in her hands, she began to walk forward over the barren grave. This time, the rods crossed as she walked over the body and uncrossed as soon as she reached the top of the grave site. Debe backed up and stood on the center of the grave. This time, when she held the single rod in the air, it slowly turned to face the foot of the grave, indicating that the person buried there was a male. We cannot prove that the body buried there is that of Pete Spence, but there is a good chance it is.

Through the years, Debe Branning and the MVD Ghostchasers have explored the Globe Cemetery during numerous Cemetery Crawls and dowsing demonstrations and have attended several of Globe's annual Historic Cemetery Walks that include costumed reenactors telling the sad tales of residents' demise. But over the years, they have found the area looking toward the hillside to be quite active, as though it might be some sort of a portal to the other world. On more than one occasion, guests to the cemetery and paranormal team members have witnessed something in the form of a dark, shadowy, cloudy mass moving across the hill from left to

A stroll through the historic Globe Cemetery. *Author's collection.*

right. Some people have even described the phenomenon as a tall man in a black suit and top hat.

One afternoon, Debe, Megan Taylor and Maria Wright made a stop at the cemetery to explore the artwork on the historic grave markers. They placed a digital recorder in the truck bed to record while they walked up the roadway. When they returned, they switched on the recorder to play it back and were stunned. On the recording devise, they heard a man speak using the Victorian English dialect of the early 1900s: "Fine witches, I see" were the eerie words discovered on the recorder.

There is definitely something supernatural happening among the tombstones in the old Globe Cemetery.

Globe Cemetery
328 Hackney Avenue
Globe, AZ 85501

PINAL CEMETERY

The historic Pinal Cemetery is a sprawling cemetery bounded by Main Street, Golden Hill Road, Fourth Avenue and North Arbor Avenue in Central Heights, located about halfway between Miami and Globe. In its early days, Pinal Cemetery was owned and managed by a small local mortuary, but the county took it over in 1918, when it sadly learned that more space was needed to bury victims of the Spanish flu.

The cemetery actually comprises four different cemeteries in one location. It reaches from flat land to high, hilly ground, accented by foliage and evergreen trees. Strolling through the cemetery, one can sense the importance of this hallowed ground. The most notable graves of famous historical figures are those of:

- Pearl Hart: The lady outlaw famous for robbing the Globe-to-Florence stagecoach, earning her the nickname of the "Stage Coach Bandit." She later settled in the Globe area with her rancher husband, George Bywater.
- Chief Talkalai: He served as chief of scouts for three U.S. Army generals and lived to be 113 years old.

Of course, there are members of many other prominent families buried here, including early land developers, ranchers, miners and cattlemen. There are legends and stories of murders and saloon brawls that ended here at the Pinal Cemetery without a grave marker left to tell the story. In some instances, single graves were used to contain more than one person, as stacked graves were a common practice in the Pinal Cemetery.

The grave marker of Pearl Hart. *Author's collection.*

Chief Talkalai is buried in Pinal Cemetery. *Author's collection.*

It's strange how you can learn about two spirited people from completely different walks of life, such as Pearl Hart and Chief Talkalai, and find them buried no more than one hundred yards from each other in the same graveyard.

Folks who make the trek in the cemetery late at night report seeing shadows moving about the tombstones and mysterious balls of light floating along the paths of this important but often bypassed historic cemetery.

Pinal Cemetery
Golden Hill Road
Central Heights, AZ 85539

8

SCHOOLS

GLOBE HIGH SCHOOL

Construction for the current Globe High School began in 1913 and was completed in 1914. The school housed about 250 students from seventh grade through twelfth grade. It was a two-story building complete with a basement and was known as a state-of-the-art facility in its early days. The residents of Globe were proud of the attractive new school when it was dedicated in 1914.

At one time, high school students attended classes at Central School, which was originally called Hill Street School. It was located near G Hill. As Globe's population began to grow, the early school became overcrowded, forcing the construction of a new, larger facility. The new school was located near the center of town. Students could easily walk to and from school, hurry home for lunch and still have time to converse with their classmates on the school grounds before classes resumed in the afternoon.

In 1920, a third floor was designed by architects Trost and Trost. This addition helped accommodate the growing number of junior high school–age students in the area. This time, a cafeteria, a garage and locker rooms were added down in the basement. There were additional accommodations made for a caretaker to live on site and for a nurse's office to be located on the main floor.

The first Globe-Miami football game was played in 1924. This was the beginning of a major rivalry that led to the creation of the G and M Hills in each town in 1934. The competitive rivalry game to win the Copper Kettle Trophy was played on Thanksgiving Day until 1965. Later, Arizona's football season was changed so it was played on an earlier date.

The high school expanded into other new buildings. In 1949, the tennis courts made way for a gym and a cafeteria. In 1956, a new junior high school was built, providing more space for the needs of the high school. Music and shop wings were added in 1964. Globe High School was renovated in 1991, and today, it is one of the oldest buildings in Arizona continuously used for education. One of Globe's graduates, Rose Mofford, became Arizona's first female governor.

As is the case for many schools, the century-old Globe High School has its share of ghosts. None of the spirits are known to be malicious. They are simply spirits lingering behind, still needing to learn lessons inside the historic mining town school.

Former students and some of the school's employees have told stories of seeing a young seven-year-old boy wearing a child's sailor suit that likes to bounce a ball against the wall of the gym. They also mention an elderly janitor who can still be heard "sweeping, sweeping with his broom." They also warned that if you are in the building late at night, you can hear the footsteps of someone walking around in circles on the second floor.

Debe Branning contacted Stacy Waddell, a longtime teacher at Globe High School. Waddell shared a few of the ghost stories that have circulated around the school over the last couple of decades. She has had several ghostly encounters since starting her teaching job at the high school in 2003. During her second year of teaching, Stacy was assigned to instruct yearbook and photography. She inherited two more classrooms, the yearbook office and the dark room, which consisted of three rooms. The front room of the dark room was more of a sitting room. It had a refrigerator and chairs inside it. Then there was the film room and the picture processing room. An old-school radio complete with an old fashion dial was inside the picture room. The class could only tune in to about three radio stations. Several times, they were in the room when all of a sudden, the dial on the radio would start to scroll up and down the stations. Other times, the radio would just turn on or off by itself. Stacy would bring her lunch every day and keep it in the refrigerator in the sitting room. She always drank a Diet Mountain Dew in the morning. Occasionally, she would forget her drink at home, but it still seemed that every time she would absentmindedly go back into the sitting

Globe High School. *Author's collection.*

room to get it, the refrigerator door and freezer door would be open. One time when Waddle reentered the room, the radio was blasting, but she had just been in the room a minute or so before.

Other experiences had by students involved the old paper towel dispenser that was never used. It had a metal hand crank on it and would begin to crank on its own while they were in the pitch dark trying to put a film on reel. They could hear the sound of tapping feet, like the tapping of impatience, because a student couldn't get their film on the spool.

Unfortunately, during a spring break, the sprinklers on the school's front lawn were left on, and it flooded the dark room. The classroom was a disaster and had to be renovated. Toward the end of the renovation, Stacy only let the editors-in-chief work there. At this time, they were two female students. All of a sudden, they came running out of the room, screaming. Stacy came to their rescue and asked what was going on. Frightened, they said there was a crazy noise like a sizzling, crackling and popping. Stacy went in the room to check things out with them. They didn't hear any noises until they started to exit the room and it began to make the sound again. This time, they all ran out.

The yearbook staff would often stay late working on a project, sometimes until 11:00 at night. During the late-night hours, they would hear doors slamming shut on the upper levels. They also heard the laughter of a child, and lights would sometimes flicker. In recent years, Waddle has seen a little boy peeking into her room during class. She has seen him three times in a period of two years, and other students have seen him, too.

In 2009 or 2010, Stacy told a friend about some of their classroom experiences. She had friends in Tucson who operated a paranormal investigation team. With permission, they arranged for the team to come to the school and conduct a paranormal investigation. They did not tell anyone else about the ghost search so that it would not leak out to the students, who would probably try to scare or prank them. The investigation team consisted of Waddle, two other women and two men. They brought cameras and put out recording devices to capture EVPs in the gym since this was one of the hot spots where people said they saw the little boy.

They placed a basketball in the center of the gym. The group decided to go to the auditorium and take more photographs there. While they were in the auditorium, a medium in the group sensed that a man in a tie was standing on the stage. Stacy believed he said the man's name was Steven. He said Steven was a calm man. They all photographed the area and saw some images of unexplained lights. They suddenly heard a door slam shut on the second floor.

About thirty minutes later, they all returned to the gym. It was getting close to 1:00 a.m. When they entered the gym, they found that all of their equipment had been moved. The battery of the camera was dead, the EVP recording device was still running and the ball they placed in the center of the gym had somehow ended up in the corner. They propped open a door in the back of the gym with a chair to let in a little light, and now, that chair was on its side, and the door was shut.

They grabbed the recorder and placed a new battery in the camera. The group propped open the back door again and placed the basketball back in the center of the gym. The investigators decided to go into the cafeteria to get some water. They were in there for about five minutes, listening to the EVPs on the recording devices. They all heard a child's voice that sounded like it said "hello" and then laughter. When they returned to the gym, they walked into the same situation as before. The basketball was again in the corner, the chair was moved from the door and the camera battery was drained.

That was the first investigation conducted at the high school. The following year, a school activity group called the Paranormal Club was formed. Stacy said, "They made a couple attempts to stay and do an investigation—but, as you know, high school kids are skittish and play pranks on each other, so I don't feel like we got much out of any of those investigations."

Not too long ago, a teacher who was in the basement with Stacy was sitting in her classroom with a student when suddenly, a table flipped over on its side. She told Stacy what happened and mentioned her friend was a bit of an empath. Her friend visited the school and felt chills with goosebumps. The friend announced she had felt the ghost's name was Steven. Class dismissed.

Globe High School
460 North Willow Street
Globe, AZ 85501

NOFTSGER HILL SCHOOL

The Noftsger Hill School sits stately at the top of North Street in Globe, Arizona, and was once known as the North Globe Schoolhouse. The school was built in 1907, and several additions were built on to accommodate the growing mining community. In 1917, the front half of the existing structure was added, and its name was changed to the Noftsger Hill School, after Globe businessman A.N. Noftsger (the hill the school sits on claimed his name first). Noftsger made his living by supplying local miners and their families with a resource more precious than Globe's silver or copper. Noftsger purchased the area's water rights. The school that bears Noftsger's name educated many generations of Globe children until 1981, when the schoolhouse closed its doors for more than just the summer. Noftsger Hill School was officially closed. One of Noftsger Hill's most famous students was former Arizona governor Rose Mofford.

The building sat vacant for ten years. New ownership and renovations changed this landmark school into a bright, spacious and charming bed-and-breakfast. For the next two decades, visitors could reserve one of six classrooms and enjoy fabulous views of the old Dominion Mine or a breathtaking view of the city of Globe. Rooms in the front of the building provided views of the Pinal Mountains and the town of Globe. The rooms in the back looked out onto the historic Old Dominican Mine. Many former

Noftsger Hill School. *Author's collection.*

students often visited their old school for small class reunions and gatherings with friends and classmates. Today, the building waits for a new venue to take over the halls of learning.

There seems to be a few ghosts in the old building that decided to stay after school was over. Perhaps some of the students of the past prefer to visit the two-story schoolhouse in spirit form. Ghost hunters found the quiet bed-and-breakfast the perfect spot for capturing EVPs and encountering a spirit or two. It was a great location to reserve all the rooms at the inn and enjoy a weekend with a group of paranormal investigators.

For many paranormal investigators, the former bed-and-breakfast was a destination where teams could book the entire facility and become one with the ghostly former students. Debe Branning recalls one of her first visits to the former Noftsger Hill Inn.

> *Megan and I booked room 2 on the first floor and carried our bags of equipment and cameras into the room. Almost immediately, things began to happen. We sat down in a couple of rocking chairs in the center of the room to plan our strategy for the night. Megan glanced over to a leather reading chair and saw an apparition of an elderly, partially bald, white-haired man with long sideburns leaning over as if he was listening to our conversation. Then he faded away.*

Later, the pair noticed the shadow of a youngster glide down the wall near the chalkboards and linger in a corner for some time. The lobby walls and the staircase were lined with classroom photographs once captured on the front steps of Noftsger School. Megan immediately recognized the visitor in their room in one of the photographs; he was a former schoolteacher or principal.

Debe often tells the story of when she was standing near the edge of Megan's bed when a very strange event happened right before her. She glanced down to see a small, black, fuzzy mass about the size of a child's fist emerge from under the bed, punch the outside of her right foot and retract under the bed. Debe was quickly down on her hands and knees to see what was under the bed but found nothing.

The MVD Ghostchasers held one of their paranormal workshops at the Noftsger Inn in January 2009 and had every room of the building reserved. There was no way any paranormal activity could possibly slip past them. The group was able to debunk some of the previous reports of unexplained voices and lights in room 1. There is an electrical power box connected to the outer wall of this particular room, which projects an extremely high EMF reading near the bed and sitting area. This could cause anxiety and a feeling of being watched.

After breakfast the following morning, it was time to pack up and head back down to Phoenix. They stood, talking to their hostess for several minutes until one of the ladies happened to glance over her left shoulder. Out of the corner of her eye, she saw a small child dash out of the room the group had been staying in (room 3), go around the corner and run up the staircase toward the small restroom on the mid-landing. It was just another endless day of summer for the spirits at the Noftsger Hill School.

Guests asked the Inn's former innkeeper, the delightful Rosalie Ayala, if there had been any recent antics from the mischievous ghost children. She nodded and recalled a story told by two guests who had checked out a few weeks earlier.

> *The ladies had been out sightseeing and shopping during the day and stopped for dinner in Globe. They brought back a bottle of fine wine to their room and placed it in an ice bucket. They poured two glasses of wine and recorked the bottle. A short while later, the cork popped from the wine bottle. It landed several feet away from the ice bucket. The startled ladies laughed the episode off, but when it happened the second time that evening, they decided it might be a good idea to leave a light on!*

On Saturday, April 26, 2014, FOTOS (Friends of the Other Side) conducted an overnight investigation at the historic inn. They elected to stay in room 3 for the weekend, as they had learned there was quite a bit of activity associated with this room. Once they were settled in, the team set up trigger objects for an experiment. They sat quietly in the room and tried to catch a read on it there and throughout the rest of the building.

Carolee Jackson introduced herself to the spirit with her usual presentation of peace, love, respect, asking permission. She was immediately approached by a young female spirit that was about four and a half feet tall, with bobbed blond hair. Carolee asked for her name, and the spirit said, "Evelyn." When asked if she went to school there, the spirit responded, "Yes."

Evelyn began repeating "five, five, five," to which Carolee asked if she was five years old. No. Fifth grade? Yes. About that time, the spirit of a young boy stepped forward, correcting Evelyn by saying "eight" several times. Evelyn adamantly denied the eight and insisted on five. And then Evelyn said, "Paul likes to push." She demonstrated to Carolee with finger poking or firmly pushing. "In the info relay, you could sense she enjoyed telling her about Paul and what she determined was naughty behavior," Carolee stated. "I asked the young male his name, and he confirmed it was Paul and that he was eight years old. Paul said Evelyn likes to tattle and move things. Evelyn said Paul likes 'pushing' people." Carolee asked if Paul was pushing on Jen and was told "yes." Earlier, a FOTOS team member, Jen, was being repeatedly touched with firmness, as if someone was poking her, pushing on her. One could see the finger impression in Jen's sleeved arm.

Evelyn and Paul like to linger on the lower level of the Inn and will make their presence known to the innkeeper and visitors. Evelyn doesn't hesitate to peek around doors and furniture and has made herself at home. Paul tends to be shyer and often follows Evelyn around the building. After breakfast,

Noftsger Hill School's hallway. *Author's collection.*

the FOTOS team meandered around the downstairs lobby, checking out the place more thoroughly, looking for information on the spirits they had encountered. Carolee was at one end of the room, where she caught the spirits of four girls talking among themselves by the girls' bathroom. All of a sudden, Carolee heard Wendy and Jen call, "Carolee! Evelyn is here! Her picture is on the wall!" She dashed to where her excited friends were standing and pointing. There was Evelyn, standing in a classroom group picture. "I recognized her immediately."

Another event that Jen and Carolee witnessed in real time was the self-illuminating light that had been reportedly seen by other visitors on the lower level. They saw the light form, and Jen had her camera, so she started to take pictures of it. The light moved toward them, softly skipping across the floor and furnishings until it disappeared after sitting on the table for a few seconds.

Carolee recalled in her notes, "Picture 1: Light appears near floor. Picture 2: Moves toward us on floor level. Picture 3: Moved up to piano. Picture 4: Seen on table next to piano. Picture 5: Light disappears."

Ghost hunters have captured EVPs of footsteps walking across the wooden floor and, of course, the faraway voices of children. They have photographed strange balls of lights on camcorders rolling during the night, usually around 3:00 a.m. Guests have heard the faint voices of teachers instructing their classrooms.

On another occasion, Kenton Moore remembered seeing a similar light. "I woke up in the middle of the night to use the bathroom. After I had finished, I opened up the bathroom door to head back to bed. A speeding ball of light flew over my shoulder and across the room. Then it suddenly disappeared." Earlier in the evening, he had placed his truck keys on a dresser but could not find them before he settled down for the night. He searched everywhere and finally decided to continue the hunt in the morning. To his surprise, the keys were back on the dresser top, in the same spot where he had placed them the night before.

There is still that old, mysterious urban legend that the children of Globe like to share about the ghosts of Noftsger Hill School. They often say the ghost of a mean teacher still walks the hallways, and they claim the bones of the evil teacher are buried deep in the basement. Class dismissed.

Noftsger Hill School (formerly the Noftsger Hill Inn)
425 North Street
Globe, AZ 85501

9
Hotels to Die For

Chrysocolla Inn

The Chrysocolla Inn was built in the late 1800s and served as a boardinghouse for local miners. It was in use for nearly one hundred years until it found itself deserted in the 1980s. Sadly, it remained empty until the Rooney family took on the challenge of bringing the old building back and creating a gracious and beautiful vintage bed-and-breakfast.

It took seven years to refinish the original floors, doors and windows, lay new/used brick in the basement and uncover and restore the old fireplaces. The Rooneys created a colorful, relaxing garden and patio space. And the fun began with collecting antiques to furnish the rooms with an authentic, turn-of-the-century feeling.

The inn takes its name from Chrysocolla (kris-uh-col-uh), a mineral found near copper veins—and Globe is known for its copper.

In its early days, the building was known as Mack's Home Hotel. It served as a boardinghouse and dining room for visiting elites, miners, students attending school from neighboring towns and visitors to Globe for dealings with the assayer's office.

Margaret McLean purchased the boardinghouse in 1915, during Globe's boom town years. Over thirty-five mines were operating in the surrounding area and led copper production for the nation. The Home Hotel was so popular that by 1929, the McLeans added a third floor. Even with the

The Chrysocolla Inn was once a boardinghouse. *Author's collection.*

Great Depression and the closure of the Old Dominion Mine, the stately Home Hotel continued to successfully operate into the 1940s. At one time, the boardinghouse/hotel boasted fifty-three rooms. Over the next seventy years, the building changed hands many times. The McLeans finally sold it in the 1940s, and from there, the paper trail is uncertain. It still operated as a boardinghouse and small apartment building, but by the 1980s, it was not in compliance for habitation and was shut down for fifteen years.

The Rooney family took the reins in 2000 with a vision. The building had seen years of neglect, and it was going to take a lot of hard work to get it suitable for guests as an upscale bed-and-breakfast.

While the beds in each room reflect the period of the home's construction, two may or may not be tied to Globe's local lore. It is said that two of the iron beds came out of the old Sang Tai Restaurant on North Broad Street, a well-known Chinese establishment that ran from the late 1880s until 1960, when a son took over and changed its name to the Star Buffet. The beds in question were purportedly used by working girls on the second floor above the restaurant during some point of the building's history; although, much of the detail of that history has been lost.

It is also believed that the property may have been where Big Nose Kate had her boardinghouse after she and Doc Holiday went their separate ways. The history books are not clear on the facts, but an older gentleman said his mother used to manage the house and that it definitely belonged to Big Nose Kate. Historians have noted a document that states Big Nose Kate's place was off Broad Street, not on Broad Street, as many building owners have suggested.

Carolee Jackson, the founder of the paranormal team FOTOS, reported a discovery while her team spent the weekend at the Inn.

> *One late Saturday evening/early Sunday morning, after FOTOS finished one of their Globe Jail investigations, Jen, Fallon and myself headed up the street to the Chrysocolla Inn, where we had rented a room for the night. (The guys on the team stayed elsewhere.) The gals stayed in the Amethyst Room on the second floor. It was late at night. The building was absolutely silent when we returned to our room for some sleep after our investigation.*
>
> *Lying in bed, we were quietly chatting about some of the data we collected from the jail and how jazzed we were with the experiences. Then we heard heavy footsteps on the wood flooring of the second floor. The footsteps went back and forth from one end of the building to the other, even stopping in front of our door twice. We saw the shadow of feet just barely*

A Chrysocolla Inn bedframe from the brothel. *Courtesy of Carolee Jackson.*

noticeable under the door. After looking at each other with one of those "Did you hear that?" looks on our faces, we quickly opened the door and stepped out, looking to see who was outside our doorway and who was walking up the staircase. There was no one. The three of us fanned throughout the building and grounds and saw no one.

I woke early Sunday morning and thought I'd do an EVP and dowsing rod session in the second-floor sitting area. Maybe the heavy-footed stranger would come through. Was he the older gentleman in spirit that I'd met downstairs when we'd first arrived Saturday afternoon or the older woman in spirit who we met in the kitchen? No, those were heavy boot steps we were hearing, not female. Anyway, I was sitting quietly on one of the sofas, listening to the environment, when behind me, I heard a woman speaking. Very soft, almost whispery voice. As I turned to see if someone was standing behind me, that soft whispery voice spoke again, only in front of me. "Where's—?" I asked who they were and said I'd like to chat with her if she'd like. The energy shifted, she was gone and I was back in silence, as if the last sixty seconds had never happened.

A ghost cat made its appearance that weekend, as well as the weekend I stayed there after doing a MVD Ghostchasers Pinal County Jail workshop. Come to think of it, we heard heavy footsteps on the second floor that night, too. But it was a quick, brief visit, not like when us FOTOs gals heard them. Those went on for easily five minutes, which was tripping us out.

Another weekend, Debe Branning and Cindy Lee were staying in the Amethyst Room with a friend. It was a quiet weekend with very few guests. Cindy woke up in the middle of the night, hearing someone walking in the hallway and a conversation just outside their door. "I got up to see if there was someone in the hall." As she stepped out the door to explore the situation, she met innkeeper Libby Rooney in the center of the hall seating area. Libby had heard the same voices and footsteps and thought there may have been an intruder. Who is this mystery guest who arrives late in the night and disturbs the guests' sleep?

Libby Rooney told us a story about a guest, Ruben Ruiz, who once resided at the former boardinghouse in room 51 when he was a boy. He may not have had many interactions with children in the building, so he came up with his own imaginary playmate—or was he really a ghost?

I invented an imaginary friend named James. Then I had a recurring vivid dream of an old-style well. How I ever got to the well, I do not know, but I

Chrysocolla Inn's room 51. *Courtesy of Libby Rooney.*

remember falling down the well! It was as rapid as the feeling of falling just before you wake yourself up in panic. But there was no waking up. There was no panic. I was only laying still at the bottom of the well, staring up at the faint circle of light of its opening. James was always by my side at the

> *bottom of the well and assured me, "Don't worry. You're not the one who's going to die down here." In the basement of the inn, there were two stone wells. One had a trapdoor that was not a secret to anyone, but the other was under the floorboards, hidden for decades. The location of the hidden well? It was right under where our bed used to sit!*

Could there have been a boy named James who once lived near the property who disappeared down the well? Perhaps he was reaching out to Ruben so that his legacy would not be forgotten.

Chrysocolla Inn
246 East Oak Street
Globe, AZ 85501

C.F. Whitcher: Shot Down at the European (Pioneer) Hotel

The Trust Building, as it was originally identified, was located on the southwest corner of Broad and Cedar Streets. The construction on the building began in January 1906. Architect W.R. Norton designed the building, and it was completed by the end of the year at a cost of $50,000.

The grand building was constructed of red bricks, with dacite ornamentation at the windows and doors. It boasted fancy balconies, ornate cornices, corbels, carved quatrefoils and gothic-looking doorways and windows. A third-floor atrium opened to a skylight on the roof and showcased one of the few elevators in the city.

Most of the Trust Building was occupied by business and professional offices for upstanding company men. The entire fourth floor was used by the Globe Business Men's Club. The ground-level shops were popular locations for tenants and shoppers in the downtown area. The Copper Belt Printing Company made use of the basement, where the *Arizona Record* was published for several years.

It has been rumored that a system of tunnels ran under the streets of Globe. One theory mentions that the tunnel system ran from the Gila County Courthouse down to the basement of the Trust Building, acting as a decoy or private entrance to the notorious gentleman's club upstairs. This way, wives and proper citizens of Globe would not see the businessmen or government officials sauntering down Broad Street to the more risqué part of town.

The Historic Gila County Courthouse and Jail. *Courtesy of the Bullion Plaza Cultural Center.*

In 1916, the building had changed its name to the European Building. It featured medical offices, dental offices and law firms, including the office of Charles F. Whitcher.

By the 1930s, the Globe Directory showed the building was still listed as the European Hotel. The professional men were still there, and some rooms were rented out for personal lodging. In 1940, its name was changed to the Terminal Hotel, most likely because the Greyhound bus station and lunchroom were housed on the first floor. The building became known as the Pioneer Hotel in the 1960s and remained that way until a devastating electrical fire in 2005 took the four-story structure down.

Judge Charles F. Whitcher, one of the senior members of the Gila County bar, was shot and killed there on May 28, 1916, by a man named J.H. Jackson. The shooting took place in front of the European Building (later called the Pioneer Hotel) around 12:30 in the afternoon. Jackson was arrested immediately after the murder. Jackson told authorities that he killed Whitcher because the lawyer had broken up his home.

Four shots were fired, two of which went wild. One of the bullets struck the lawyer in the face, near his nose, and came out near his right ear. The other ball entered his back, just to the right of his spine and came out through his left breast, just above the heart.

As one can imagine, there were several eyewitnesses to the killing, but as in most cases, their descriptions of the tragic affair differed in detail. Whitcher had walked down Broad Street from the Dominion Hotel. As he approached the steps of the European Building, where he had his office, Jackson, who had been sitting on the steps at the tower corner of the building, stepped out toward him, drawing his revolver at the same time.

Witnesses Abe Lockwood and Robert McBroom, both elderly men, were sitting on the steps at the European Building at the time. Lockwood said that as Jackson drew his gun and stepped toward Whitcher, he said, "You will interfere in my family affairs, will you?" and then fired the first shot. Abe did not know whether that first bullet took effect or not. Robert McBroom grabbed Jackson, and in the scuffle, Jackson was thrown down the basement steps. Whitcher rushed up the steps leading to the record office and tried to get in the building, but to his dismay, the door was locked. He turned and started down the steps again. At that moment, Jackson rushed up the basement steps, gun in hand, and the two men met on the upper steps.

Whitcher, who was disabled and always used a walking stick, struck at the gun with his cane. Two more shots were fired, and Whitcher turned and tried his best to escape by crossing Broad Street toward the Old Dominion Commercial Company's store. Jackson was not about to give up. He continued to follow Whitcher and passed him. Whitcher then turned back toward the sidewalk he had just left. Standing directly behind the lawyer, Jackson took aim and fired the fourth shot. Whitcher fell forward in the gutter at the edge of the sidewalk. Jackson fired the gun again, but the cartridge did not explode. Another shot was not necessary—he had finished his deed.

Dr. H.D. Kenney, who was also attracted by the shooting, stepped forward and felt the stricken man's pulse. "There is nothing that I can do," he remarked as he stepped back onto the sidewalk.

Hearing all the noise and confusion, Deputy Sheriff W.H. Maher and Officer Floyd Blevins arrived on the scene and took hold of Jackson, who gave up his gun when he recognized the deputy sheriff. Jackson was taken to the Gila County Jail at once, and the body of Whitcher was soon removed to the Jones and Son undertaking establishment.

Jackson was interviewed at the jail later that day by a representative of the *Daily Silver Belt*. He said he did not care to say much, as his lawyer had advised him not to talk. "But I am willing everybody should know this much. My family is broken up, and Whitcher is the man that broke it up."

Jackson was willing to talk about the shooting but not about what led up to the tragedy.

> *I was sitting on the steps at the corner of the building when Whitcher came down the street. I went toward him and fired. I don't know whether that shot hit him or not. They caught hold of me, and I was pushed down the basement steps. I don't know who pushed me down. There were a number of men there. I came up and went after him again, but I don't know just how things happened. You see, they were trying to catch hold of me and were pushing me around, and I was trying to keep them off and from hurting anyone else. So, I don't know what shots hit or what didn't. I didn't want to hurt anyone but Whitcher, and I knew just what I needed to do. Finally, he tried to run across the street, and I ran around him. Then he turned to go back, and I fired another shot. I tried to shoot again, but the gun wouldn't fire.*
>
> *I have lived in Globe about ten years. I came here from Texas, and I never had any trouble with anybody before. I have always worked and paid my bills, except for a few little bills I ran last winter while working on my claims—and I am going to pay them after a while.*
>
> *That old man Whitcher wanted my claims, but he'll never get them. He was using my wife to help him get the property. I wouldn't care so much about losing the property, but it was losing my family that hurt. And he done caused it.*

As Jackson spoke of "losing his family" his eyes filled with tears, and he turned away.

Previously, Mrs. Jackson had appeared in justice court in Globe and stated that her husband had been abusing her. She said they had been married for sixteen years and that she couldn't live with him any longer and wanted to get a divorce. She was told that she would have to go to the superior court for a divorce, as such cases were not handled in the justice court. Since that time, Jackson had not been living with his family. It was noted that Whitcher was to represent Mrs. Jackson in the divorce proceedings. The papers had not been served to Jackson at the time of the killing. Jackson feared his wife was after his mining claims and that the lawyer was influencing her into awarding him some of the proceeds. Jackson's brooding troubles and fear drove him over the edge.

Judge Whitcher had been a resident of Globe for nine years and for several years had been associated with Lawyer Neil M. Alfred. Whitcher came to Globe from Prescott but was originally from New York. His wife and daughter remained in Buffalo, New York. Whitcher told his friends that his wife could not live in Arizona because of the climate and that he could not live in the East because of the climate there. He was about fifty-five years old at the time of his death and was buried in the Globe Cemetery.

When it all ended, the body of Charles F. Whitcher lay in the morgue of the Jones and Son undertaking establishment in Globe; J.H. Jackson was held in the Gila County Jail, charged with murder; and a spatter of dried blood was a sad reminder on the edge of a cement sidewalk, marking the place where one man killed another.

While the Pioneer Hotel was still in operation, staff would report hearing party revelers late at night on the top floor. Urban legend speaks of a woman who fell or was pushed from the fourth floor, but no documentation was found to confirm that. Movie theater guests next door felt strangers sitting in the seats next to them. With the new refurbished theater built on the actual sight of the old hotel, do guests still share their popcorn with an unseen guest? Take a stroll down Broad Street late at night; perhaps you will encounter the terrified soul of Charles Whitcher crossing the road, seeking a location where his life might be spared.

Pioneer Hotel (now the site of the Hollis Cinema 4 Theatre)
161 North Broad Street
Globe, AZ 85501

DEADLY AFFAIR AT THE LANTIN ROOMING HOUSE

It was a chilly January morning when a troubled Globe couple was joined in a cold, eternal death, realizing their souls would never be able to live in wedded bliss in this lifetime. Two bodies laid side by side in the darkness of the morgue—one of Mrs. Alma Brown, aged twenty-six, dead after two bullets were fired into her head with murderous intent by her despondent and jealous husband; the other of Thomas "Tom" R. Brown, aged thirty, who died by suicide, expiating his crime with the same weapon he used to gun down the defenseless woman. And somewhere in the city, so the rumor added, walked the man whose attentions to the wife angered the slayer and reinforced his determination to execute the deed, which he boldly succeeded in doing. The truth of this rumor may never be known, as a search failed to disclose any secret letters to substantiate what was current talk. Whether Brown expected to find the other man there and dispense justice, which he, in his blind passion, conceived to be his right, was up to speculation.

The tragedy occurred at 9:20 a.m. on January 17, 1911. It all took place in the two-story Lantin Rooming House, located at the corner of Broad and Bailey Streets. Alma Brown had been living there since her separation from her husband several weeks prior. Mrs. Brown was preparing to do some cooking in the kitchen, it is said, when Tom Brown came to the hallway and rang the doorbell. With no perception that beyond the entryway was a man with murder in his heart, the wife opened the door and gave a piercing scream of terror when she saw the barrel of the weapon and read the intent in her husband's frenzied eyes.

Brown fired a shot almost instantly, the bullet entering near Alma's mouth. She turned to run, and he fired again as she fled, the second bullet striking her in the side of the head, behind her ear. Neighbors heard four shots, the last being the one that crashed through Brown's brain. Both wife and husband were mortally wounded. Alma Brown passed away at 10:00 a.m., and Tom Brown lived until 11:00 a.m.

Coroner Hinson Thomas and several other people in the neighborhood viewed the bodies at the scene of the horrible tragedy. Alma Brown's body was found lying in a pool of blood in the hallway near the banister. Her husband, moaning and unconscious, was lying close to her body, the revolver nearby. The bullet that was fired into his temple had tunneled

The Max Lantin building. *Courtesy of Carolee Jackson.*

through his head and was found on the floor by the coroner. Mrs. Brown, still breathing, was carried into her room and placed on the bed, where she lived for about forty minutes. Tom Brown was left where he had fallen after someone bound some cotton over the wound, and the slowly dying man's gurgling and choked breathing became more than some of the curious crowd could stomach. The coroner decided that it would be useless to remove him to the hospital. The physicians believed he would not survive for more than an hour.

The bodies were later taken to F.L. Jones and Son funeral chapel, and messages were immediately sent to a sister of Alma and her son from a former marriage. It had been stated that before her marriage to Tom Brown, Alma was known as Mrs. Thomas Williams, a young widow. Originally from Georgia, Alma came to Globe with the Ina Lehr Theatrical Company, and her marriage to Brown took place on February 23, 1909, after only a two-week acquaintance.

Tom Brown, a Scottish immigrant, came to Globe in 1907 with other members of his family from the town of Clifton. He was engaged in business, first with his brother, George, and later employed at the White House Saloon. He eventually owned the cigar stand in the Old Iris Theater Building, where he probably met Alma. He was a member of the Odd Fellows.

The ghost sign at Lantin's. *Author's collection.*

It was apparent that the murder had been contemplated and planned for some time. Brown had recently purchased the revolver from the Globe Hardware Company. In his clothing were found two rounds of ammunition besides that which was still in the chamber of the weapon. Some local informants said that the cause of the separation was Brown's ill treatment of his wife; while others attributed it to different reasons. It was understood that Alma Brown was running the Lantin Rooming House, which she was buying from Mrs. Leonard with multiple payments.

Brown had tried many times during the recent weeks to effect a reconciliation with his wife, and neighbors stated that quarrels were frequent between the two of them. Brown had suffered financial losses, and his health had turned for the worse. In the dead man's pockets was a very significant letter that read as follows:

> *Dear Brother—You may think this is strange for me to go this way, but the jig is up with me—so don't worry, for it will be better now than later, so good bye! Take my house and sell it. Mrs. Gibbs has my book. Get it, and you will see what to do. Lon Sanders owes me $50.00. Get it, sell out the rooming house and get your money out of it. The lease is in the Old Dominion Bank.*

The bodies of Tom Brown and Alma were consigned to their last resting places side by side in the old Odd Fellows Cemetery in Globe. Reverend John M. Burnhart presided over the services. He told the mourners, "Only God knows the measure in which the husband and wife were free. Only God knows the secrets which are buried with their bodies. It is not man's prerogative to judge his fellow men."

Lantin Rooming House (former site)
396 North Broad Street
Globe, AZ 85501

THE DELACY HOUSE

The red-brick DeLacy House was built around 1910, and like many of the buildings on North Broad Street, it was said to have been in the red-light district. Prescott resident Ada DeLacy came down to Globe and married

The DeLacy House. *Courtesy of LeeAnn Powers.*

Jerome DeLacy in 1897. He ran the saloon on the main floor while Ada ran the upstairs hotel. The couple divorced in July 1909 and had one son named Lee. With Jerome DeLacy out of the picture, Ada later remarried William A. Sprague, who was also in the saloon business. Their hard work made the DeLacy House a popular boardinghouse, and it was advertised as a hotel with "nicely furnished rooms." It was located over the Roosevelt Stage Office.

Ada DeLacy later moved to Los Angeles with her only son, Lee, who dabbled in the film industry.

This location is often visited on the yearly Ghosts of Globe haunted tours, and legend states that a soiled dove (or lady of the night) died in one of the rooms in the upstairs brothel.

There was a gentleman by the name of A.G. Hayes who was arrested at the DeLacy House in November 1917, fined $200 and sentenced to serve ninety days in the city jail for beating his wife. His sentence was suspended, and he was asked to leave Globe. Perhaps some of that brutal energy still lingers in the building.

Spirits of a man and a woman have been spotted on the upper floors of the building. Sometimes, only the top portion of the woman is seen, while only the legs are visible on the man. And poof—just like that, the couple is gone.

On the ground floor, there was once a saddle shop operated by a gentleman by the name of White. Mr. White resided in the rear of the shop. Today, there is a bathroom in that area with two doors. Once, a male customer went into the bathroom and locked both doors. They were promptly pulled open by some unseen force. Mr. White apparently did not like locked doors. The spirit is also known to turn on lights. Although it is no longer a working hotel, one of those nicely furnished rooms is just waiting for you.

Site of the Former DeLacy House
410 North Broad Street
Globe, AZ 85501

10
Saloons and Brothels

Spirits of the Drift Inn Saloon

The Rabogliatti family arrived from Italy and settled in Globe shortly after the early 1900s. They constructed a six-thousand-square-foot building that was one of the largest structures on Broad Street. The building was divided into three sections, or bays, with three entrances to separate the businesses. The south end of the building was home to the Club House Café, the middle section was the location of the notorious International Saloon and the north end of the building housed a business called Western Cash. There was a sign near a stairway leading to the second story of the building that read "International Rooms," and those stairs led to a prosperous brothel.

The madame had the largest room near the top of the stairs. The sex workers plied their trade in the twenty cribs that lined the long hallways. It was known to be one of the finest brothels in Globe. Downstairs, the International Saloon had a reputation, too—wild and dangerous. Miners, cattlemen and cowboys came from miles around to celebrate their successes and belly up at the bar. Loaded pistols were placed every few feet along the thirty-foot-long bar for use of the bartenders in case things got out of hand. There were several gaming tables for faro and poker. A raised platform above the back door housed an armed guard, who watched over the activities of the saloon.

The Rabogliatti building. *From Wikimedia.*

Businessmen Dominic and Alfred Rabogliatti raised their families in a living quarter at the rear of the International House. The two brothers celebrated the joys and tragedies of their families all within the noisy backdrop of a bawdy barroom. Over the years, the building has been occupied by several other businesses. It has housed a barbershop, restaurant, grocery store, furniture store and music store. The saloon has changed ownership several times as well. It has been known as the Owl Bar and Blackie's Tavern, and in 1980, it became the Drift Inn Saloon.

The former owners of the Driftwood Inn greeted the MVD Ghostchasers outside of the building in 2003 and related how they came to purchase the saloon. The prospective buyers were passing through Globe on a road trip when they decided to stop and have a drink at the Drift Inn. It was for sale, and they had a good feeling about the building—as though it had a special aura about it.

They opened a side door that led the MVD Ghostchasers to the second floor of the Rabogliatti building. The now silent hallways were once buzzing with ladies of the night entertaining the gentlemen from the saloon. Now, the upstairs floors of the building are active with ghosts. Both men and "the ladies" have been seen up there in the back hallway. A cowboy specter

The Drift Inn's staircase to the brothel. *Author's collection.*

roams in silence as if searching for someone. The legend says a jealous early-day cowboy came looking for his girl upstairs in one of the rooms of the International, where he maliciously shot and killed her.

To this day, an unsolved murder continues to haunt the upstairs brothel. A young miner by the name of Joseph Ludwig was not known to be a lady's man, but he was often seen in the company of certain women from the tenderloin district. The 190-pound man was a gambler and lost most of his payroll earnings playing faro. Late in October 1907, he lost more than just another paycheck. Ludwig lost his heart—and not in a romantic way.

Many of the working ladies of the tenderloin district were hired at the International Saloon as "bar rustlers." Innocent male patrons of the saloon were often doped and seduced upstairs to one of the rooms in the brothel. Once the door to the room was closed and the man was passed out on the bed, the crafty women would quickly search the victim's coat and pants pockets for money, jewelry and anything else they could find of value. When the unsuspecting gentlemen came out of their stupor, often embarrassed or unsure of what had just occurred, they sheepishly snuck out the back door, never telling a soul where he had been.

It is assumed Joe Ludwig was hustled up to room 18 by one of the ladies of the International Saloon as well. Whether the motive of his death was greed, self-defense or a twisted love affair (perhaps an angry woman's act of revenge), it shall never be known for sure. But at some point, during the night, Joe Ludwig's throat was ripped open with a sharp blade, and his heart was carved out of his chest. His limp body was then carried out of the hotel and taken about a mile to a deserted canyon. He was blown up in an attempt to destroy the evidence of the crime. His broken body was found with a bloody towel wrapped around the neck, his severed heart on the ground about thirty feet away.

Bloodstained sheets and bed clothing identified the body and indicated that Ludwig's throat had been cut in room 18 of the International Rooming House. It was also learned that he had suffered a minor stab wound a few days prior to his murder. Was one of the ladies working in the brothel possessively jealous? Did she decide to put an end to his wandering eye? It was said there was a custom in Southern Europe to cut out the heart of a man who had disrupted the family of another.

Just one year later, in November 1907, another tragedy occurred upstairs in room 18 at the International Hotel. Even though the second crime did not seem as horrific or bloody, there was something so uncanny that a possible connection between the two crimes was traced. If the musty walls of room 18 could talk, the tales of two vicious crimes could possibly be solved.

One Sunday afternoon, the body of Richard Vecklund, a young twenty-five-year-old Finnish miner, was found in the bed in room 18. The chambermaid discovered the remains around 2:00 in the afternoon and notified the authorities at once. Strangely, this was the same chambermaid who testified in the Ludwig case one year earlier. A postmortem examination showed Vecklund had come to his death by poisoning. His lungs were badly discolored, and his heart was clogged with blood that had turned black in his lungs. His stomach was sent to San Francisco for chemical analysis.

Saturday night, shortly before midnight, two Globe police officers came across a young man standing in front of a sporting house in the red-light district. He appeared to be intoxicated to the point that he seemed like he had been drugged. He opened his eyes, and the officers asked where he lived. In a weak voice, he whispered, "Room 18, International." Confused, the police officers escorted him to the hotel, where he was taken and put to bed. What possessed Vecklund to say, "Room 18, International?" His friends indicated that he did not have a room there. They reported that he was residing at the Central House on Broad Street, four blocks away. Was Vecklund in some mysterious manner implicated in the Ludwig crime and in his drugged condition gave that answer because the effect of the drug brought back to his benumbed brain a recollection of the earlier crime?

Earlier that evening, Vecklund went to the tenderloin district with his companions. They confirmed he had over one hundred dollars in his pockets. When he was picked up, unconscious, by the officers, he had no money on him. The crime itself was easily explained. Vecklund was undoubtedly given chloral, or "knockout dope," in his drink by some inhabitant of the tenderloin district and robbed. There was probably no intent to cause his death, but he died from the effects of the drug. There was small probability of the guilty ones getting caught, and they escaped the penalty—forever.

Back down in the saloon, the owners told the paranormal investigators they had seen an old man or cowboy in a gray suit standing behind the bar, and they said he would sometimes drift off into the kitchen and storage room. He often stood behind unsuspecting customers, looking over their shoulders without saying a word. When the surprised customer would reach out to the man, he would simply disappear into thin air. Could he be one of the Rabogliatti brothers overseeing what is remaining of his American dream? Or is he a customer from the saloon's wild past stopping by to quench his thirst?

Barstools are knocked over for no reason. Billiard chalk has been seen flying through the air. Owners often blame these things on the ghosts. The bartender told us that a spirit from the past will occasionally call out his name. All these things occur when there were no patrons in the bar.

Could the man be the victim of the famous Globe Christmas Eve Killer of 1944? Or is it the gentleman who was shot by his ex-girlfriend in 1963 as he sat on a barstool at the end of the bar?

Debe Branning and Cindy Lee participated in a paranormal investigative tour of the Drift Inn led by Amy Schrader, the previous director of Arizona Ghost Adventures. The group was led upstairs to the haunted brothel area, where they visited a number of rooms that are noted to have paranormal activity. The hallways and empty rooms looked much like they had one hundred years ago, with wooden floorboards, painted carpet flooring, misnumbered doors to vacant hotel rooms and just a touch of a few modern conveniences, since the current owners used them as living quarters.

The group sat in a circle in one of the rooms to test various ghost hunting equipment, such as the SB7 spirit box, a paranormal puck and dowsing rods.

Right: Was this the notorious room 18? *Author's collection.*

Below: The busy Drift Inn Saloon. *Author's collection.*

Moving on to the next room, the investigators gathered to do an EVP session with digital recorders and pendulums. As the group stood or sat in this large room, Cindy signaled Debe to look inside the connecting room. They stood and watched as the door at the opposite end of the adjoining room began to open slowly, as though someone had come from the other world to see what the visiting investigators were up to. They watched for several minutes as the atmosphere in that room began to feel heavy with an unexplained energy. Debe and Cindy excused themselves from the group and walked into the adjoining room to test for air flow and to see if another guest had wandered in that direction. Nobody was there.

The tour group gathered in one last room for more experiments. Debe and Cindy walked out to the main hallway, where a gentleman was setting up his SLS camera to scan for movement in another room. They stood out in the hallway and focused on one room that was used as storage. It had its window boarded up, and the walls and floors showed bare wood.

"Walk in here," Cindy coaxed. "Tell me what you feel."

Debe walked into the deserted room and stretched out her arms, trying to get a feel for the uneasy energy. After a minute or two, she stepped back out, shaking her head. "Something bad happened in this room."

Cindy nodded. "I really think so, too. I feel this is the deadly room 18."

Debe shook her head and looked around the room. "I think you are absolutely correct. It feels so unsettling in there!"

They had no doubt that this was room 18. The energy was dark and oppressive, and both ladies had a sick feeling in their stomachs. A couple of years later, Travel Channel's *Ghost Adventures* was back in Globe to film an episode at the Drift Inn. Using some of Debe's historic research, the show featured the haunting of those murdered in room 18. Debe showed the film crew the room the ladies believed was room 18, the death room. The show later placed Aaron Goodwin in the crude, vacant room, where he experienced despair and anxiety beyond his control.

Although the doors and the room numbers have been changed throughout the years, the residual energy left behind by those unsolved murder cases continue to be the heart of the mystery. The owners of the saloon insist they are on good terms with the ghosts. Just don't be surprised if you see or hear an occasional inexplicable spirit from the past—and "that ain't the liquor talking."

Drift Inn Saloon
636 North Broad Street
Globe, AZ 85501

The Fashion Saloon

The Fashion building, located on the corner of North Broad and Hackney, housed the Fashion Saloon. It was built by its owners, Giacoma and Bracco, in 1909. The lower floor was occupied by the Fashion Café and the Fashion Saloon and Bar. The rear of the building sported a very popular electric garden with lawns for the Italian men to play boccia. The second floor was the lodge hall for the Lega Fratellanza, an Italian organization that supported the lodge, the Italian community and the W.L. Human Rights Lodge no. 339. The lodge hall was rented out to miners and various organizations for meetings and dances.

Seeing as the saloon was situated on the rougher edge of town, it was often the scene of gunfights, stabbings and fistfights. Once again, there was a brothel ready to serve the local cowboys, miners and businessmen on the second floor.

Robert E. Merritt, forty-four years old, drove his vehicle off the bridge at McCormick Wash on Pine Street, just behind the Martin Theatre on September 11, 1921. Tome Nixon and Walter Doolittle later found him

The entrance to the former Fashion Saloon. *Author's collection.*

unconscious and laying on the sidewalk in front of the Fashion Rooms on Broad Street. He was carried inside and put to bed in a room upstairs. Apparently, Mr. Merritt woke up in the middle of the night and saw the light from the window. Not knowing where he was, he walked through the glass window and fell two stories, landing on his head and cracking his skull. He was taken to the county hospital, where he died several hours later. The inquest jury agreed that it was an accidental death. He was buried in the Elks plot of the Globe Cemetery.

The upstairs area of the Fashion building has recently become an active location for paranormal investigations. Vincent Amico of the Arizona Paranormal Investigations and Research Society has started to add periodic tours and investigations on the second floor, where traces of the old brothel and lodge hall can be found.

Amico noted that the hallway leading to the bathroom seemed quite busy and that one of the guests was touched. Fresh flashlight batteries died in the old upstairs brothel rooms, and the rooms themselves gave everyone an uneasy feeling.

The groups have heard voices speaking in Italian upstairs. Due to the fact that it was a lodge hall for a good portion of the Italian population of Globe, one can only hope the messages will soon be studied and translated. Using trigger objects, Vincent Amico and his crew have contacted a spirit of a child named Michael who tends to be seen or heard on the righthand side of the staircase or toward the back of the building.

Be on the lookout for future tours of the Fashion building, and become one with the past.

The Fashion Saloon Building (various merchandise shops)
610 North Broad Street
Globe, AZ 85501

11
Fraternal Organizations

Elks Lodge

The Elks Lodge boasts a spot in Ripley's Believe It or Not! as the world's tallest three-story building. The legend states that the number of bricks needed for the construction of the building was somehow overestimated, so the builder simply continued to add the bricks until they were all used.

In 1899, a group of business and professional men in Globe decided to petition the state to organize a local lodge of the Benevolent and Protective Order of Elks. "Distinguished Elks from around the state met in Globe and organized Globe Lodge 489. Officers were elected, and sixteen men were initiated into the order." The Globe Elks met in temporary quarters for over ten years and made plans for a building of their own. On March 20, 1910, the cornerstone was laid for the new headquarters on Mesquite Street.

The lodge was built by D.A. Evans in a Romanesque style. The three-story building is forty feet tall by one hundred feet wide. The first story featured a large, arched entryway. A decorative balcony highlighted the second level. There were arched windows on the third floor that were shaded by a massive cornice at the top of the façade. It still has its high ceilings and now houses Globe's Antique Mall.

Initially, the Elks used the upper two stories for their lodge meetings and functions. The ground floor had many commercial purposes. The Elks Theater (later called the Iris Theater) provided social entertainment for the citizens of Globe.

Right: The Elks Lodge building was featured in Ripley's Believe It or Not! *Author's collection.*

Below: The Elks Lodge building's cornerstone. *Author's collection.*

There is a ghost that roams the building and is believed to be the first Exalted Ruler of Lodge 489. He has been known to open locked doors and turn on the lights in the bar and has been heard walking upstairs and in the first-floor hall. Former bartenders noted that the light in the hall at the head of the basement stairs would often turn on by itself. They would hear someone on the basement stairs, but upon investigation, nobody was there.

Many years later, a large plaque listing the early leaders of Elks Lodge 489 was found half buried in mud in the basement of the Elks building. Miraculously, it was saved and is now on display at the Globe Train Museum.

Clifford Welch was found dead in his room one morning at the residence of Mrs. Morton. He was a member of the Globe Lodge of Elks and had participated in the first ceremonies of the lodge the previous Saturday night. A friend accompanied him at the gate around 2:30 a.m. on Sunday, when he was apparently in good health and spirits. On Sunday morning, about 8:00, groans were heard coming from this room, but no one, it seems, entered to check on him and see if he was OK. The unfortunate man died alone, probably during the afternoon of Sunday.

Acting coroner Whalley held an inquest over the remains, and a verdict of death from heart disease was rendered. It was said that the man was subject to heart spams. F.L. Jones, the undertaker, received a letter from Welch's mother stating that his father had died from heart disease as well and that this was something the ill-fated young man inherited.

Clifford was a comparatively young man and of quiet disposition. He had been a resident of Globe for only six or seven months, having come from Jerome. Undertaker Jones took charge of the body, and the funeral was conducted by Globe's lodge of Elks from the Odd Fellows Hall. The services were impressive. Mr. A. Jacobs delivered a brief speech, in which he dwelt on the many good qualities possessed by the deceased. As is customary with the Elks, the band played a dirge, led the cortege to the Globe Cemetery, where the beautiful service was concluded, and all that was mortal of Clifton Welch was consigned to its last resting place.

Jones Mortuary occupied a workspace in the basement of the Elks building for several years, along with a first-floor storefront and office space. Having access to the alley, the funeral parlor found it convenient to store or move corpses in a discreet manner there. Urban legend states that in the early 1900s, local young people would break into the mortuary. There were so many bodies that the funeral director had to stack them upright. This frightened the intruders so badly that they ran all the way home.

Left: A large, old plaque was found under the mud in the Elks Lodge basement. *Courtesy of Carolee Jackson.*

Right: The alley behind the Elks Lodge building. *Author's collection.*

One Halloween, Debe Branning and a group of friends, including Cindy Lee, Tamara McGinnitty, Sandy Thompson, Gloria Pinkerton and their friend who was visiting from Australia, Rachaelle Gaultier, decided to attend the Ghost of Globes walking tour, a two-mile jaunt past some of Globe's most haunted sites, complete with ghostly costumed reenactors describing their lives and deaths in early Globe.

They strolled through the streets and approached the Elks Lodge. As they stopped to hear another spooky biographical story, Cindy noticed a spirit of a man standing by the nearby corner street sign. He watched the tour group for a minute or two, enjoying the tales, and then he slowly faded away into the darkness. They continued walking down a dimly lit alley and passed by the locked entrance to the old mortuary. Debe noticed the doorknob to the closed door of the building was slightly turning back and forth, as though someone was on the other side. She stopped in her tracks to take a second look. Cindy nodded, as she had seen the unexplained movement, too.

Later, after the tour had ended, the ladies wound down for the night after a few dances at the Drift Inn. The group of costumed ghost hunters decided to take one more drive along the dark, deserted alley next to the

Elks Lodge before they called it a night. The streets were quiet now, and one could hear a pin drop.

As Cindy drove slowly up the alley, she began to roll down the automatic car window to listen for any unearthly sounds. This caught Rachaelle, who was riding in the front passenger seat, off guard. An ear-piercing "scream queen" shriek was heard, and it surely woke the dead. They could not help but burst into laughter. Rachaelle thought for sure something was about to grab her in the desolate alleyway.

A word of caution for those who wander down the darkened alleys of Globe late at night: You just may encounter an Elk—and not the sort you may find in the forest.

Elks Lodge Building
155 West Mesquite Street
Globe, AZ 85501

12
Tales of Mystery

Webster House

Fred Beck, an old-time Globe miner, aged fifty-eight, died by suicide one early Sunday morning at the boardinghouse known as the Webster House. The despondent man was said to have shot himself with a 30-30 rifle early that morning.

Coroner Thomas was notified, and soon, an inquest panel jury consisting of W.D. Kendrick, J.I. Bolton, T.J. Helton, J.D. Meyers, Harold Shute and William Henderson was gathered together. The inquest was held on Tuesday morning at the office of Coroner Thomas. In the testimony of several witnesses, they told of the pathetic fact that Mr. Beck felt he was becoming old and could no longer find stable, hard work. The anxious man had become overwhelmingly despondent, and the jury rendered the following verdict: "That Fred Beck came to his death about five minutes after four from a gunshot wound in the head, self-inflicted, with suicidal intent."

One of the peculiar features of Beck's suicide, which was brought out at the inquest, was that no one in the Webster house had heard the shot. Mrs. Mark Brookenshire, however, testified to the fact that she had heard a shot at 4:05 on Sunday morning.

Beck left a brother, Charles Beck, who also resided in Globe, and two other brothers, who were residents of Iowa.

The Webster House was the scene of deadly encounters. *Author's collection.*

But the story doesn't end here. Fred Hansen and his wife, Bethena, had been married for twelve years. Sadly, for the past year or two, the couple just had not seen eye to eye. The arguments grew to be too many, and Fred had recently been arrested for threatening the life of Bethena. They parted ways—he went back to the farm, and Bethena stayed in town and rented a small two-room cottage with their three children behind the Webster House.

One afternoon, Fred came by the cottage to pay a visit to the children and before long the conversation between the couple grew intense. Knowing that their marriage was over, Fred pulled out a .41-caliber Colt revolver and fired two shots at Bethena. One bullet penetrated her left breast, and the other tore a hole in her left cheek, passing through the back of her head. Either would have been fatal.

As his wife sank back in her chair, dead, Hanson placed the gun to his own head and fired a shot into his right temple. Death was instantaneous. Mrs. Hanson's sister heard the shots from next door and raced to the cottage, fearing disaster. There was nothing more to do. Their oldest son, who was ten years old, had witnessed the gruesome scene. The boys were raised by Bethena's parents in Tonto Basin.

And then there was another mystery at the Webster House location. When Paul Michaelson moved into the Old Miner Boardinghouse above the Webster House, he did not know the move was going to net him $300 before the week ended. Nobody owed him that amount of money, and he didn't know of any way to earn it in less than a week, but it happened!

There was a rumor that an area of the front yard had recently been beautified when what happened to Paul became known. There also may have been some backyard beautifying as well, with some folks stating, "He tried to improve the looks of things, even under the house."

It all happened because Michaelson appreciated beauty and neatness. When Paul moved into the new place, he had plans to create a pretty yard. He secured shrubs and bushes and began to dig. As he was digging a hole for a lilac bush, his spade struck something. It hit whatever it was several times, and when it was through striking it, Paul had $300 worth of silver ore piled up—actual buried treasure right in the front yard. He did not waste any time cashing it in.

It was said that one of the old silver smelters was located on the present site of Michaelson's home and that the cache was probably deposited in a part of the dump. There was much surprise, however, that a find of such high-grade ore could have been made. But is there more?

Webster House (This is a private residence—do not disturb!)
Globe, AZ 85501

The Miracle on Willow

A horrific explosion nearly destroyed the home of Alfred and Dominic Rabogliatti, the proprietors of the Globe Theater, on November 2, 1922. This act is said to have been the most evil, inhumane and violent ever committed in the town of Globe, and it was committed against the Rabogliatti family. Alfred and his wife lived in one side of the duplex with their three children. Dominick and his wife lived in the opposite side of the structure with their four children—this meant eleven family members were living in the same home.

The two families were sleeping soundly in their beds on Willow Street that Thursday evening. They all believed their new home was quite lovely, as it was originally a one-family home. It was quite spacious, and the floorplan allowed it to be remodeled into two separate living spaces. There were two entrances, two bathrooms and two kitchens. The families were very close and shared the same yard and garden—they even shared the same automobile and theater.

On the night of the frighting horrors, Alfred and Dominik had finished their work at the Globe Theatre and arrived home shortly before midnight. Soon, everyone was safely asleep in their beds—or so they thought.

The only warning the family had came from Alfred's four-year-old son, Eddie. About an hour before "The Blast," as it came to be called, Eddie, who didn't frighten easily but had a lively imagination, entered his parents' bedroom and woke them. He insisted that he had seen a man in a black coat and black hat walking around the house, dragging a long rope behind him. They should have listened, but they shrugged it off as one of Eddie's tall tales.

Alfred Rabogliatti recalled what happened that fateful night.

> *The first thing that I remember hearing Eddie say was, "Daddy, I'm afraid." I told him to lie down and go to sleep. Once again, he repeated the same words—but in a louder tone. I asked him what he was afraid of. Finally, he climbed out of his own bed and came into the room occupied by myself and wife. He jumped right on my bed and crawled over me. As he had never done anything like this before, it naturally attracted my attention a little, but of course, I did not anticipate anything like what happened later on.*

He continued. "I asked him, 'What is the matter with you?' I couldn't quite understand his answer, but I now remember he said something about something or somebody being about the house."

They told the boy, "Don't be silly. There is no man walking around the house. Go back to sleep."

Having been awakened at an early hour, Mr. Rabogliatti did not pay a great deal of attention to the whims of a four-year-old boy. He noticed that the boy was really frightened, and he thought it would be best to let the lad remain in their bed. It was a good move, as his bed was destroyed in the blast.

Boom! Suddenly, at 2:45 a.m., the house exploded. The windows shattered, walls collapsed, furniture was broken, water pipes burst and the floors fell into the basement. As one can imagine, the terror and confusion was horrifying. Alfred managed to keep it together and shouted to his family, seeking a head count. Sirens blared as the fire department and police arrived at the scene.

Alfred Rabogliatti explained, "A little while later, we heard the noise of the explosion." The next thing he recalled, he was rising up in the air. He

The house on Willow Street was nearly destroyed by dynamite. *Courtesy of the Rabogliatti family.*

struck his head on the ceiling, cutting a small wound in his scalp about one inch in length. Then he fell on top of a mass of wreckage. He must have been unconscious for a short period. When he came to, he found a lot of broken pieces of furniture and wood and plaster around him. Later on, he found a lot of wooden splinters in his clothing.

He then related how he heard cries coming from under the debris. He discovered that his wife was under the wreckage and beneath the floor as well. She was not injured and passed up one of the children to Mr. Rabogliatti. She had quite a difficult time getting Eddie out of the mass of rubble, but she at last succeeded in passing up the youngster, who had been so frightened just a few minutes before.

"I asked my wife, 'Where is the other baby?'" The frightened woman told him that try as hard as she could, she could not reach the baby. At last, the baby, who was nearly two and a half years old, crawled from under the floor on his own accord.

Mr. Rabogliatti said that all the while it was very dark and they were in their night garments, their regular clothing, including their shoes and stockings, were gone. And of course, they could not find their shoes if they wanted to. They had to feel around the massive wreckage the best way that they could, barefooted and guided by a lighted candle.

One of the children remembered being wrapped in a blanket and carried to the safety of the garden, where he was handed off to a neighbor.

Everyone in town, all dressed in nightwear, searched for them. Slowly, each child was found and transported to safety. Neighbors brought blankets to keep the family warm in the chilly night air. Fortunately, the parents were not seriously hurt.

Faust, aged six, had been sleeping in the front room of the house. They could hear him crying for help, and both parents tried to get to him. It was difficult at first. The house had been wired for electricity, as it had been their custom to use electric lights. Groping in the darkness, everything seemed to be topsy-turvy. Alfred finally succeeded in finding the place where the electric light button was and turned on the switch, only to find that all the connections were broken, except those in the front room, where little Faust was crying for help. When they finally succeeded in getting to him, they found he was trapped under a safe that was placed in the house for the purpose of storing valuable documents. Faust was found alive, but for perhaps two hours, his young life hung by a thread—or more accurately, a floor joint. He had dropped through the floor of his bedroom and was wedged bleeding between two water pipes. The massive overturned safe rested only inches from his head, held there precariously by a two-by-six-inch piece of wood.

They couldn't even move the safe until some of the neighbors came to help. Together, several of the strongest men in town tried to lift the safe. Not being able to brace their bodies properly, they were unable to budge the awkwardly shaped and heavy safe. It kept slipping out of their grasp over and over again.

Suddenly, a very large man, who no one in town could ever identify, appeared on the scene, lifted the safe and held it in his mighty arms just long enough for the others to free the young boy. The mysterious man of extraordinary strength did not stay around very long in order to be thanked. Did he need to hurry off to help with the next miracle on his list?

When Faust was rescued, it was found that his right arm had been broken and he had a cut on his head where the safe had hit him, but it was not thought his injury was serious. He carried a scar over his temple for the rest of his life as a reminder of his brush with death.

Concerning the rescue of Dominic's family, Alfred added.

> *Dominic stated that he had been awakened by the blast. When he tried to turn on the electric lights, they did not respond. Later, he found that the water pipes were broken, and water was flowing in the bedroom. His first thought was to search for his wife and children. His wife had not been injured, but the bed had been damaged. They both began searching for their*

> *four children. They had no problem finding three of them, Katherine, Neal and baby Adolph. The baby was just three months old with a fragile body. He was not hurt, except for a scratch on his nose. His metal buggy, placed nightly at his parent's bedside, where he slept, was smashed flat. He was found lying on the well-padded foot of their bed. Members of the family have said, "If there were logical explanations for miracles, they would not be miracles."*

But little two-year-old Alfred, who had been sleeping near the window, had been blown through the opening and landed outside. His bed had been situated along the side of a French window facing the empty lot. The window's glass had blown out as well as part of his bed, and he landed on a rock six feet from the empty lot.

The search was on for young Al, and it caused everyone much despair until a tiny woman arrived at the home carrying the unconscious two-year-old in her arms. The woman was the wife of a miner who was on the graveyard shift, and she had been sleeping in bed when she heard the explosion. Fearing the worst, she arose to find out what had happened just down the road. As she made her way across the shadowy lot, she stumbled and nearly fell on the boy's crumpled body.

The boy lay pale and motionless for two days at the Gila County Hospital. The doctors prepared the family for the worst, thinking he might not survive or have brain damage. But the youngster made it through his injuries and lived a long life.

The family stayed in temporary housing while the duplex on Willow Street was being restored—and there it stands after many renovations through the years. They all moved back into the home, and after some time, the worry on their faces disappeared.

But how and why did this all happen? The how was easy to determine. Fragments of sticks of dynamite placed under the floor were found on one side of the house. But the why was a little more difficult to comprehend in this mystery puzzle. They began to think carefully. Who were their enemies? The judge gave them a clue. "Look to your own kind," meaning the Italian community. The family pondered the situation a little more.

The dynamite was placed directly under the large safe. The safe remained undamaged after the blast. Inside was Joe Blessenti's last will and testament (see chapter 6). As you will remember, Blessenti had a niece who lived with him whom he spoiled outrageously. Although she presented herself as a little angel, that was not so true. She was not popular with the other ladies in

The Dynamite House. *Author's collection.*

town, and they loved to gossip about her. Even though Blessenti treated his niece to a finer life in Globe, his final will and testament did not say she would inherit his wealth; rather, it was to go to his family in Italy.

One of the girl's admirers was a nervous young fellow who didn't seem very bright, and although she used and abused him, she was able to mesmerize him. After "The Blast," her suitor quit his job at the mine, became increasingly pale and shaky and spent most of his waking hours drinking in the saloons. It was said that during one of his drunken ramblings, he reported that the niece was the one who duped him into participating in the plot to blow up the house in order to break into the safe and destroy the will. There was never enough evidence to press charges against either of them. In time, the tormented man found a way to escape his guilty conscience. He shot himself in the head. The niece moved away, and the family eventually moved back into their rebuilt home.

The joke was on the devious, plotting couple. The will had been taken out of the safe to be recorded and executed and placed in a desk. It was located intact in one of the desk drawers of Mr. Rabogliatti's home. All the greed, destruction, anxiety and fear were played out for no reason.

The mysterious man who rescued the young child from the falling safe was never identified. Some believe he appeared out of nowhere, like some strange, unknown phenomenon or perhaps an angel from the heavenly skies. But what they did conclude was that the near tragedy was the miracle they would never forget!

Willow House
Private Residence
Globe, AZ 85521

GEORGE HERAKLIDES: THE SWAMI OF GLOBE

A stranger materialized in the town of Globe in the early months of 1916. Nobody knew who he was or where he had come from. All they knew was that he was very charismatic and mesmerizing with his wisdom and peculiarities. His name, Heraklides, alone drew a crowd—and it should have—his former history was something out of another world.

He arrived in the United States in 1892 and began a wrestling career under the guidance of promotional manager Charlie White. Heraklides was mocked by opponents, who stated he looked like a peddler off the street due to his thick, matted head of hair and mustache. White groomed the young scraper and began matching the strapping five-foot-six-inch, 170-pound, twenty-four-year-old man with some of the best wrestlers on the East Coast.

Charlie White soon had Heraklides competing in New York City at Madison Square Garden in a match against Mr. "Puff and Grunts" Yousouf, the Terrible Turk. The Turk won the first fall in forty-seven seconds on a half nelson. He twisted the Greek's neck in such a manner that Heraklides was unconscious for a half a minute. The Greek was able to go on fourteen minutes later. The Turk won the second fall and the match in one minute and ten seconds.

Luck was not in the cards for another important bout between Heraklides and a Japanese wrester by the name of Takezawas. The match was held for a purse of $5,000. There were to be three bouts, but at the end of the first round, Heraklides was badly winded, and his huge chest and abdomen rose and fell with heavy respiration. Just one cigarette stood between Heraklides and collapse. Heraklides was a heavy smoker and could take almost half the combustion of a whole cigarette into his

Early Broad Street. *Author's postcard collection.*

lungs with a single inhalation. Before the match, he had smoked one cigarette, eaten an orange and drunk two glasses of ice water. It did not take long for the "Strong Jap" to bring the "Terrible Greek" to his knees. Heraklides went to the mat, and his body began jerking with convulsions. Every muscle in his body knotted, and he foamed at the mouth. The referee drew Takezawas away from the unconscious Greek. Heraklides did not rise. The match was awarded to Takezawas. Heraklides was left in an extremely dangerous condition and barely survived.

After it was decided that his wrestling expeditions should come to an end, the enterprising showman took on new ways to entertain old and new audiences. In 1901, Heraklides was in Chicago, where he opened an office for the purpose of teaching people how to attain strength such as his. He originated the pyramid trick and held sixteen men on his shoulders at one time. During the world's fair, he was connected with Buffalo Bill's Wild West Show and performed many seemingly impossible feats of strength. He proclaimed he had been born in Greece and that his father was a Corinthian doctor and his mother a Bedouin. Early training developed Heraklides into a muscular giant. When he was young, he could lift and throw boys twice his age. Heraklides was a proponent of vegetarianism and physical culture. His theories were obtained from his physician father and observations among the Bedouins.

George married a theatrical actress by the name of Minnie around 1892, and together, they had nine children, three of whom had survived to the 1910 census. The couple later separated, and Minnie had to take Heraklides to court in order to obtain money to support herself and the children. The headline read "He of Long Hair and Supernatural Powers Failed to Provide for Wife and Children Held for Trial." Minnie claimed that they argued and that he left her at the house with no money. She went to the streets and picked up junk and sold it so she could get money to buy food and clothing for the children.

Heraklides waltzed into the courtroom, wearing high boots and a black cutaway suit. His hair fell in dark, shiny curls on his shoulders. His mustache was long, and his beard was shaved, except for a black streak around his mouth. He told the judge he did not send money because he could not even support himself. Minnie announced to the court that he never made less than seven dollars a day when he told fortunes—sometimes more. Heraklides was insulted when the judge asked him if he was a fortuneteller. He boldly insisted that he was an astrologer. I bet he did not predict that the judge would put him on parole for two years for failure to provide for his wife and family.

In July 1915, Heraklides was arrested for practicing medicine without the obligatory authority of the medical board and was sent to jail. Later that year, the Light from the East gave lectures on the Holy Land. Seer George then claimed he was born in America, raised in India and traveled the world for twenty-five years. Shortly before arriving in Globe, Heraklides was noted to be in Deming, New Mexico, around July 21, 1916. There, he claimed to be a descendant of Alexander the Great. He professed the Buddhist religion and said he could cure many of the ills to which the human family is heir. His treatment consisted of massaging and the use of the Hindu bath. He also claimed to specialize in respiratory disease.

Heraklides lectured on Eastern philosophy and the occult sciences. He was a man of superior intellect and refinement and was well versed on thought transference and mental telepathy. He also dabbled in astrology and other mystic arts. In addition to his love for the occult, Heraklides was a student of medicine. The swami, as he was sometimes called, performed miraculous cures for which he refused to accept remuneration. His lectures on the religious practice of the East had incurred for him the enmity of the followers of Buddha around the country.

It may have been the transgression of the rules of faith that brought about the untimely end of the seer through the medium of some unknown Eastern poison. Perhaps he should have taken heed of his own medicine—or perhaps it eventually became the misfortune of his being. His life suddenly ended on a hillside in the lower part of the city of Globe on August 12, 1916. He was found half buried in the weeds and garbage on the hill behind the old Miners Union Hall around 12:00 p.m. His body was discovered by the driver of the ice wagon who lived a short distance from the spot where the corpse was found. He noticed a splotch of white on the hillside, which, upon investigation, proved to be the remains of the "Indian philosopher."

An odd feature of the affair lay in the fact that Heraklides was seen at 9:00 a.m. that same morning by a number of people. At that time, he was apparently in the best of health and very cheerful. When Coroner Hinson Thomas examined the body of Heraklides just three hours later, rigor mortis had already set in, and patches of his skin were falling from his arms. He was guessed to be about fifty-five years old. An inquest was held in the afternoon at the office of Judge Hinson Thomas. It was noted that the seer had died from a cyst on his brain. He was buried in plot 20B of the pauper's field at the Globe Cemetery.

Did the magical swami put a whammy on the town of Globe to hold in paranormal energies for all eternity?

Globe historian Kip Culver—"Gotcha Last!" *Author's collection.*

Paranormal Resources: Teams and Tours

Arizona Desert Ghost Hunters: www.adghosthunters.com
AZ Ghost Adventures: www.azghostadventures.com
AZ Paranormal: info@AZParanormal.com
AZ Paranormal Investigations and Research Society: www.azpirs.com
Crossing Over Paranormal: www.thecopscrew.com
Friends of the Other Side: www.friendsoftheotherside.org
Ghost Hunters of Southern Tucson: www.facebook.com/groups/2468619340062334/?ref=share
Ghost to Ghost Arizona: www.ghosttoghostaz.org
MVD Ghostchasers: www.mvdghostchasers.com
Phoenix Arizona Paranormal Society: www.phoenix-arizona-paranormal-society.com
Phoenix Ghost Tours: https://phxtours.com/ghos t-tour
Phoenix Haunted History Tours: marshallshore@gmail.com
Southern Arizona Scientific Paranormal Investigators: www.SASPI.org

BIBLIOGRAPHY

Anderson, Donna. *History of Globe Arizona*. Seattle, WA: Classic Day Publishing, 2007.

Arizona Daily Star. "Man Shoots His Wife and Then Kills Himself." February 16, 1911.

———. "Sarah N. Sorin Woman Lawyer Dead at Globe." May 1, 1914.

Arizona Record. "Brothers Unite After 18 Years." August 27, 1916.

———. "Dynamite Ruined Home Year Ago." November 2, 1923.

———. "Globe Machinist Meets Solitary Death at Work in Repair Shop." November 18, 1921.

———. "Indian Swami Dies Mysteriously on Hillside in Lower Party of City." August 13, 1916.

Arizona Republic. "Assassination in Gila Jail." July 4, 1911.

———. "Fate of Woman in Globe Murder Case in Hands of Jury." October 20, 1923.

———. "New Crime for Globe." June 26, 1911.

———. "Women Cheer When Globe Waitress Is Released on Bond." April 7, 1923.

Arizona Silver Belt. "A.J. Murton's Awful Fate." July 26, 1906.

———. "Bakery Building Completed." January 17, 1909.

———. "Deadly Affair at the Lantin Rooming House." January 18, 1911.

———. "Despondent Beck Kills Himself." December 6, 1911.

———. "Dies from Drug After Robbery in Tenderloin." November 11, 1907.

———. "E.F. Breyer Is Killed at Globe." November 18, 1919.
———. "Elks Lay Corner Stone." March 22, 1910.
———. "F.L. Jones." July 13, 1899.
———. "Fred Beck Kills Himself by Shooting." December 6, 1911.
———. "How It Feels to Be Dynamited." November 2, 1922.
———. "Negro Fiend Shoots Down Wife and Flees to the Hills." October 3, 1909.
———. "Noftsger Hill Has Its Own Halloween Stories." October 22, 2003.
———. "Skeleton of Woman Found by Miners Near the City." March 29, 1908.
———. "A Suicide." May 29, 1902.
———. "Three Miners Injured." January 25, 1906.
———. "U.S. Mediator McBride Dead; Result of Accident." October 9, 1917.
———. "Would Be Murderer Suicides After Act." October 5, 1909.
Bisbee Daily Review. "Baker Caught in Dough Machine, Is Crushed to Death." December 4, 1920.
———. "The Bridge of Sighs at Globe." July 22, 1917.
———. "Three Injured by Bomb Blast at Globe, Ariz." November 3, 1922.
Branning, Debe. *Arizona's Haunted Route 66*. Charleston, SC: The History Press, 2021.
———. *Dining with the Dead*. Phoenix, AZ: American Traveler Press, 2017.
———. *Grand Canyon Ghost Stories*. Helena, MT: Riverbend Publishing, 2012.
———. *The Graveyard Shift*. Phoenix, AZ: American Traveler Press, 2012.
———. *Haunted Phoenix*. Charleston, SC: The History Press, 2019.
———. *Sleeping with Ghosts*. Phoenix, AZ: Golden West Publishers, 2004.
Copper Era and Morenci Leader. "Bodies Lay Side by Side in Grave." January 27, 1911.
———. "Pneumonia Is Cause of Mrs. Sorin's Death." May 8, 1914.
Deming Headlight. "A Relative to Alexander the Great." July 21, 1916.
El Paso Herald-Post. "Jumps to Death to Escape Prison." May 3, 1912.
Enss, Chris. "Wild Women of the West: Sarah Herring Sorin." *Cowgirl Magazine*, October 20, 1985.
Graham Guardian. "Charged with Brutal Crime." June 28, 1911.
Haak, Wilber A. *Globe's Historic Buildings*. Globe AZ: Gila County Historical Society, 2006.
Haak, Wilber A., and Lynn F. Haak. *Globe*. Charleston, SC: Arcadia Publishing, 2008.

Hernandez, John. "A Christmas Murder in Globe: The Owl Buffet Saloon." January 15, 2018. www.CopperArea.com.

———. "Walking Amongst the Ghosts of Globe." February 19, 2018.

Morning Union. "Brothers Lost to Each Other for 18 Years Are Reunited in Mine Shaft." October 3, 1916.

National Labor Tribune. "John McBride Dead." October 18, 1917.

New York Evening Journal. "Heraklides to Wrestle Yousouf." June 11, 1898.

Rabogliatti family. "The Miracle of Willow Street." Diary used with permission.

Sain, Wilma Gray. *Miami: A History of the Miami Area, Arizona.* Valdosta, GA: Aakenbaaken and Kent, 2017.

Tombstone Weekly Epitaph. "The Globe Robbers Lynched." August 26, 1882.

Tucson Daily Citizen. "Clues Are Lacking in Globe Mystery." November 1, 1906.

———. "Murderer Awaiting the Gallows Tries to Suicide." March 18, 1908.

———. "Olds Is Killed Through Jail Cell." July 5, 1911.

———. "Sheriff Averts Lynching at Globe." June 28, 1911.

———. "Woman May Have Figured in Horrible Tragedy." October 20, 1906.

Vega, Santos C., PhD. *Around Miami.* Charleston, SC: Arcadia Publishing, 2011.

Weekly Journal Miner. "Murders Daughters of Mining Partner." June 28, 1911.

About the Author

Debe Branning has been the director of the MVD Ghostchasers, a Mesa/Bisbee, Arizona–based paranormal team, since 1994. The team conducts investigations of haunted and historical locations throughout Arizona and has offered paranormal workshops/investigations since 2002. Debe has been a guest lecturer and speaker at several Arizona universities and community colleges, science fiction and paranormal conferences, historical societies and libraries.

Her television appearances include features on an episode of *Streets of Fear* for FearNet.com (2009); an episode of Travel Channel's *Ghost Stories* about haunted Jerome, Arizona (2010); and on an episode of *Ghost Adventures* titled "Old Gila County Jail and Courthouse" (2018). As a paranormal journalist, she has investigated haunted locations, including castles, jails, ships, inns and cemeteries, and has taken walking ghost tours in the United States, England, Scotland, Ireland and Mexico. She has been the guest of the Historic Hotels of the Rockies and U.S. Tourism Departments in Carlsbad, Salem and Biloxi.

Debe is the author of *Sleeping with Ghosts: A Ghost Hunter's Guide to Arizona's Haunted Hotels and Inns* (2004), *Grand Canyon Ghost Stories* (2012), *The Graveyard Shift: Arizona's Historic and Haunted Cemeteries* (2012), *Dining with the Dead: Arizona's Historic and Haunted Restaurants and Cafés* (2017), *Haunted Phoenix* (2019), *Ghosts of Houston's Market Square Park* (2020), *Arizona's Haunted Route 66* (2021) and a series of three children's books, The Adventures of Chickolet Pigolet (*The Bribe of Frankenbeans*, *Murmur on the Oink Express* and *You Ought to Be in Pig-tures*).